A Psycho-Theological
Exploration of
New Testament
Concepts

E. Basil Jackson, MD, PhD, JD

AN IMPRINT OF
GLOBALEDADVANCEPRESS

A Psycho-Theological Exploration of New Testament Concepts

Copyright © 2015 by E. Basil Jackson

Library of Congress Publication Control Number Data:

Jackson, E. Basil 1932 —

A Psycho-Theological Exploration of New Testament Concepts

ISBN 978-1-935434-67-2

Subject Codes and Description: 1. PSY012000 Psychology: Education and Training 2. REL102000 Religion: Theology 3. PSY029000 Psychology: Reference

Cover design by Global Graphics
Cover Photograph by Gloria G. Green

Printed in Australia, Brazil, France, Germany, Italy, Spain, UK, and USA

The Press does not have ownership of the contents of a book; this is the author's work and the author owns the copyright. All theory, concepts, constructs, and perspectives are those of the author and not necessarily the Press. They are presented for open and free discussion of the issues involved. All comments and feedback should be directed to the Email: [comments4author@aol.com] and the comments will be forwarded to the author for response.

Order books from www.gea-books.com/bookstore/ or boldbog@aol.com.
or anywhere good books are sold.

Published by

POST-GUTENBERG BOOKS

An Imprint of GlobalEdAdvancePRESS

TABLE OF CONTENTS

PUBLISHER'S PREFACE

The need for an integrative work by a classical scholar, trained in both psychology and theology, has been longstanding. E. Basil Jackson, with multiple doctorates and years of practice as both a Theologian and a Psychotherapist, was well equipped to produce such a work. Using available classical literature and the Greek New Testament, Dr. Jackson made comparisons with Hebrew and Old Testament references in an interpretive exploration of psychological and theological concepts.

Diligently searching for early writings that adequately defined the initial terminology, Dr. Jackson, avoided the more recent works that moved away from the original intent of the early writers with more humanistic influence and perhaps influenced by atheistic concepts of anthropology. The ultimate objective of this work was to produce a psycho-theology in summary form.

This book makes a detailed examination of various concepts related to both psychology and theology utilizing both secular and religious sources. The foundational construct is that the concept of soul is of Greek origin. Consequently, Dr. Jackson made a conscious effort to formulate a concept of soul which was both psychologically and theologically meaningful.

This work is a significant contribution to both integrative and interpretive theology with informational value for individuals working in the systematic structure of theories concerning the relation of conscious and unconscious psychological processes. Also, those working in the field of religion will find the book an enlightening read.

-Hollis L. Green, ThD, PhD, DLitt

Chapter I

INTRODUCTION

There is a great need in both the fields of the behavioral sciences and theology for systematic research into the correlates of psychology and a sound Biblically based theology. The majority of psychological theories appear to have been formulated on the basis of humanistic if not downright atheistic concepts of anthropology, and it has been on the foundation of such theories that the popular systems of psychotherapy and even pastoral counseling have been built. Very little serious attempts have been made to integrate psychological and theological concepts by theologians, and virtually none by evangelical theologians, and even less by psychologists or psychiatrists.

This has been, undoubtedly, true because of the great paucity of workers who are trained or competent in both fields, and because of the length of training involved such a shortage is not difficult to understand. It is imperative, however, that this vacuum be filled since it is only on the basis of a sound Biblically based anthropology that a Christo-centric psychology and theory and practice of behavioral change can be produced.

To build such a system the first step must be to make a thorough examination of all the pertinent vocabularly and concepts in both fields and on this basis to attempt a Biblically

1

based integration. The common practice, when theologians and psychologists meet, seems to be for them to engage in prolonged discussion without ever deciding on a definition of the terms they are using. Dialog without specific definition, however, turns out to be parallel discourse with a meeting possible only at infinity.

The Method Employed

In keeping with what has just been expressed an attempt will be made to examine and define a number of psychological and also theological concepts. Upon this basis of specificity an attempt will be made to formulate an integrated system. In this connection, it is most important to note that extensive use will be made of models and particularly of the psychoanalytic model of human personality. This is not to imply that this model is, in any way, to be considered as the "best" or the "right" one. Much trouble has arisen between behavioral scientists in the past because some have forgotten that the model is only a model, a tool, and must never be confused with reality. Any model is only "right" when it satisfies the need for which it was created and in this particular case that need is to help the observer describe and perhaps explain the phenomenal world of his client. Clinical experience has long demonstrated that the model is for the therapist's benefit and is actually of little concern or interest to the patient. This author is also convinced that human personality, as it comes from the hand of the creator, is far too complex to ever be explained completely by any one model and that when any observer, whoever he may be, proclaims that he has discovered the model, then he is merely announcing his ignorance.

A similar word of caution might well be sounded regarding the concept of energy which has been found useful in tackling the admittedly difficult and complex phenomenology of human personality. There is a discussion in Chapter III as to how Freud must have been introduced to and attracted to such a notion, and an examination of basic psychoanalytic theory certainly demonstrates that He found it most useful. It is important to remember, however, that Freud used the concept merely as an analogy as he struggled to understand phenomenology, and he was content to use it as a mere analogy until he thought of a better one. It is also true that he hoped that one day, as a result of more advanced technology, psychic energy might be a measurable entity. However, even if that should prove to be a false expectation, as long as the notion is seen to be nothing more than analogy, it serves a purpose.

The whole concept of conscience in both secular and religious authors will be examined in detail. The psychologic aspects of conscience will emphasize the psychoanalytic notions since more has been written within this frame work than elsewhere in psychological literature. Against the back-drop of the structure of the psychic apparatus there will be a detailed examination of the development of the Superego and the fine distinctions between the Superego and the Ego ideal will be discussed. The concept of conscience in secular Greek literature will then be examined as well as its use in both the Old and New Testaments. With the information discovered in these pursuits an attempt will then be made to examine some significant passages in the Greek New Testament where the concept of conscience occurs and to see what exegetical insights may result from the psychological theories which have been examined.

There will similarly be a detailed examination of the concept of soul in both secular and religious works with stress being placed on that fact that the common notion was, in the main of Greek origin. The use of the word soul in the Old Testament, the inter-Testamental Period and also the New Testament will then be examined. Since psychology says little or nothing about the concept of the soul an attempt will be made to examine the use of the word in the Bible to formulate a concept which is psychologically as well as theologically meaningful.

The concept of spirit is also examined in the same manner with emphasis being given to the use of the word in the Old and New Testaments as well as in secular and post-Biblical Greek literature. The concept of energy will be used in seeking to understand the Biblical notion of spirit and it will be seen that such a concept finds some basis in Biblical revelation.

The final chapter will be an attempt to produce a psychotheology in summary form. A psychotheology of man's conscience, soul and spirit will be offered and this will be used in examining the common prevailing notion's of man's constitution. Man as created in the image of God will also be considered as will the subject of the psychotheological events associated with regeneration.

Chapter II

CONCEPTS OF CONSCIENCE

Conscience is a phenomenon which may be considered from many different viewpoints. The philosopher devotes himself to considering whether conscience is an emotion or a function of the reason. The psychologist directs his attention to its association with particular instincts characteristic of the human species. The anthropologist traces its emergence from the group-morality of the primitive tribe. The historian elaborates the theme of the growth of liberty of conscience in western civilization.[1] To these various questions some attention will be given, but the main purpose is to examine the psychological theories of conscience or Superego, particularly that of the psychoanalytic school, and to attempt to correlate the findings with the New Testament concept of conscience.

On the whole, modern psychology, especially that of the academic in contrast to the clinical variety, appears to be quite reluctant to use the word conscience or to discuss the concept. An examination of the leading works on psychology of the past century, beginning with Spencer's new psychology, reveals that many more psychologists have failed to use the word conscience than have used it.

---

[1]K. E. Kirk, Conscience and its Problems (London: Longmans, Green & Co., n.d.), p. 3.

6

There is no discussion of conscience in Spencer's Synthetic Psychology, and surprisingly enough, none in William James. Of course, one would not expect to find it in the behaviorists, and a perusal of at least two of the most commonly used and in many ways excellent recent psychologies, reveals that there is no reference to the word. Here again would seem to be a situation where art, literature, business and religion unite in demanding, for practical purposes, a human trait or quality which psychology refuses to discuss, certainly without which human nature cannot be understood.[2]

There are, however, some exceptions to this reluctance to examine conscience. In 1893 Baldwin[3] discussed various aspects of conscience in considerable detail. He stressed that the imperative function of conscience was to make the individual feel right after he has discovered what constitutes the right. He also enumerated various laws of conscience stressing that conscience can be strengthened by repetition of conscientious actions and that it works in the light of intelligence.

McDougall[4] discussed the then popular notion that conscience is a divinely planted organ whose function is to differentiate between right and wrong. He comes out very plainly against any theory of an innate moral sense or conscience and pointed out that the older moralists who favored such a view had never sufficiently taken into account how the individual's ethical sense is, at least

[2]W. Emerson, Outline of Psychology (Wheaton, Illinois: Van Kampen Press, Inc., 1953), p. 428.

[3]Joseph Baldwin, Elementary Psychology and Education (London: Appleton and Co., 1893), pp. 241-253.

[4]William McDougall, Character and Conduct of Life (Boston: Putnam, 1927), p. 148.

in some measure, impressed upon him from his milieu. It is
only when the individual is considered in artificial abstraction
from his social relations that one needs to postulate some special
innate faculty.

Thorndike[5] likewise discusses the phenomenon of conscience
and surprisingly, in view of his experimentalist orientation, he
considers it as one of the possible instinctive endowments. He
does not go so far as to state that conscience is the basis of
the religious instinct, but he does concede "the universality of
certain phenomena." He is also prepared for criticism of his
position and discusses some of the specific criticisms which he
anticipates and he stresses that he does not postulate an innate
difference of response to "right" and "wrong" acts. Thorndike
is careful to point out that he takes this particular position
in spite of the opinions of a majority of students, such as, for
example, Lloyd Morgan, whom he quotes as saying:

> Among civilized people conscience is innate. In-
> tuitions of right and wrong are a part of that moral
> nature which we have inherited from our forefathers.
> Just as we inherit common sense, an instinctive judge-
> ment in intellectual matters, so too do we inherit that
> instinctive judgement in matters of right and wrong
> which forms an important element in conscience.[6]

Vaughan,[7] who has perhaps more to say than most psychologists on the subject, regards conscience as developing out of

[5]E. L. Thorndike, Educational Psychology (New York:
Columbia University, 1913), p. 202.

[6]Ibid., p. 204.

[7]F. W. Vaughan, General Psychology (New York: The
Odyssey Press, 1939), p. 272.

social approval and disapproval. He feels that a categorical imperative is formed in each individual because ideas of right and wrong are inculcated by environmental approval and disapproval.

Woodworth[8] has expressed rather succinctly his views on the origin and functions of the conscience. He says that by identifying with the authority the child becomes an authority himself. The code which was initially imposed on the child later becomes his own personal code of right and wrong. Woodworth also points out that the process of identification at first is with parents and family and later will also be extended to include aspects of the social group.

Carmichael[9] is very non-commital as to the nature and origin of conscience, but he does admit the importance of the subject. He points out that mere knowledge of right and wrong does not ensure right conduct but stresses that some such knowledge is a prerequisite of character, even though not a guarantor of it.

Freud more than any other psychologist has attempted to examine and understand the phenomenon of conscience. A large portion of this study in psychotheology will be devoted to an examination of Freud's ideas and formulations so in this introductory section a basic statement of what Freud himself said relative to the topic will suffice. Speaking of the conscience, which he also called the "censor" or "superego," Freud says:

---

[8]R. S. Woodworth and D. G. Marquis, Psychology (New York: Henry Holt and Co., 1947), p. 141.

[9]L. Carmichael, Manual of Child Psychology (New York: John Wiley and Sons), 1946, p. 739.

I also told you that by analysis of the narcissistic disorders we hoped to gain some knowledge of the composition of the ego and of its structure out of various faculties and elements. We have made a beginning toward this at one point. From analysis of the delusion of observation we have come to the conclusion that in the ego there exists a faculty that incessantly watches, criticizes and compares, and in this way it is set against the other part of the ego. In our opinion, therefore, the patient reveals a truth which has not been appreciated as such when he complains that at every step he is spied upon and observed, that his very thought is known and examined. He has erred only in attributing this disagreeable power to something outside himself and foreign to him; he perceives within his ego-----an ego-ideal, which he has created for himself in the course of his development. We also infer that he created this ideal for the purpose of recovering thereby the self-satisfaction bound up with the primary infantile narcissism, which since those days has suffered so many shocks and mortification. We recognize in this self-criticizing faculty the ego-censorship, the "conscience"' it is the same censorship as that exercised at night upon dreams, from which the repressions against inadmissible wish-excitations proceed. When this faculty disintegrates in the defusion of being observed, we are able to detect its origin and that it arose out of the influence of parents and those who trained the child, together with his social surroundings, by a process of identification with certain of these persons who were taken as a model.[10]

In contrast with the psychologists, theological and para-theological writers generally have given serious consideration to the whole phenomenon. Delitzsch,[11] for example, considers it sufficiently important to give it a section in his Systematic Theology. He notes that conscience, which is a native faculty of every human being, is most difficult to understand and that it has too often been wholly neglected in works on anthropology

---

[10]S. Freud, _A General Introduction to Psychoanalysis_ (London: Liveright, 1935), p. 371.

[11]F. Delitzsch, _A System of Biblical Psychology_ (Edinburgh: T. T. Clark, 1867), p. 92.

and psychology. He notes that when Kant presented what has
come to be the time-honored threefold division of the immaterial
part of man as intellect, sensibility and will, he failed to
include conscience. He describes conscience as sitting in
judgment whether an action be good or bad.

Delitzsch discusses at some length the origin of
conscience:

> A wide range of opinion exists respecting the conscience.
> At one extreme lies the contention that conscience is an
> acquired attitude of mind, a mere habit formed by the disci-
> pline of early training, which training accenturated the
> values of good and evil. The acid test of this opinion is
> somewhat brought to light by uncivilized people who have had
> no moral ideals held before them. Since conscience is capable
> of being weakened and seared, it could be expected that what-
> ever may have been its native strength in the early childhood
> of heathen peoples, it would be all but destroyed as one's
> years advance. At the other extreme lies a conviction that
> conscience is the voice of God speaking directly in the human
> soul. A test for this theory to pass would be the evident
> fact that conscience is capable of being weakened and wholly
> defeated--tendencies which are not easily associated with
> the actual voice of God. The Bible assumes the presence of
> conscience in man as a native factor of his being and predicates
> such limitations of it as to make it a fallible human charac-
> teristic. Though subject to weakening through abuse, conscience
> is presented in the Scriptures as a monitor over human actions.
> It seems to be something inborn and universal rather than an
> acquired faculty and to be a voice of human origin rather than
> the voice of God.[12]

Delitzsch feels that conscience is not a development, but
is an innate endowment. Commenting on Paul's concept of "the law
written on the heart" (Romans 2:14-16) he points out that the law
is not conscience but that conscience is consciousness of that law.

---

[12]Ibid., pp. 163-165.

He writes:

> Thus conscience gives witness to that inner law in
> man in his own sight (summarturei), impels and directs
> man to act according to that law (the so-called precedent
> conscience), judges his doings according to this law
> and reflects his actions and his circumstances in the
> light of this law (the subsequent conscience): not as
> though the conscience were a special spiritual activity
> associated with the will, the thought (judgement),
> and feeling; but it is the effectual power in the spiritual
> forms of activity concerned in those internal experiences.
> From the side of this critically judging and condemning
> activity, the conscience is conceived of in reference
> to one's own doing. (Heb. 10:2), and in reference to
> the doing of others (I Cor. 4:2, 5:11). The conscience,
> therefore, is the natural consciousness to man, as such,
> of the law in his heart; the religious moral determination
> of his self-consciousness dwelling in the human spirit,
> and effectuating itself even against the will in all the
> forms of life of man; the ethical side of the general
> sense of truth (sensus communis), which remained in man
> even after his fall; the knowledge concerning what God
> will and will not have; manifesting itself progressively
> in the form of impulse and judgement, and feeling.[13]

Similarly, he states that conscience is not the voice
of the Holy Spirit speaking directly to the soul. Rather it
is an actual consciousness of a divine law established in man's
heart. The conscience cannot, in effect, be the voice of God
in man for conscience is a subjective idea and not a correlative
one. It is not God which gives witness to the conscience but
the conscience which gives witness to man (II Cor. 1:12). The
view is not well established in Scripture, that the conscience
is the reflex of an immediate self-evidencing of God in man and
still less that it is this self-evidencing itself. Delitzsch
stresses that conscience in its primitive form was exactly
knowledge knowing itself in God. In consequence of the fall,
however, it became a painful consciousness of the lack of unity

---

[13]Ibid.

between the two. Today it is no longer the perfectly true mirror of God's law in man but still exists there as the ineradicable dowry of its divinely constituted nature.

Sajous[14] takes the position that conscience is the internal voice of the Divine Spirit and feels that every living soul has an illumination of God in the sense of the internal voice of the Holy Spirit. He also stresses that this is not a special heritage of any one race, creed or color.

Foster speaks of conscience as "a new biological organ of man" and quotes Hocking at some length as follows:

> My own view is that conscience stands outside the
> instinctive life of man, not as something separate,
> but as an awareness of the success or failure of that
> life in maintaining its status and its growth. It is
> a safeguard of the power at any time achieved. It
> interposes a check when an act is proposed which threatens
> "integrity." What conscience recognizes is that certain
> behavior increases our hold on reality, while certain
> other behavior diminishes that hold, constitutes what the
> old Southern Buddhist called an asava, a leak. The remark
> of conscience is that course, or that act, promises to
> build, or threatens to tear down, what you metaphysically
> are. Conscience is native to human nature in the sense
> that it is within the capacity of human nature to be thus
> self-conscious in perceiving and controlling its own cosmic
> direction. It is not an instinct. It is the latest and
> finest instrument for the self-integration of instinct.
> And it is an instrument characteristically human.[15]

Foster then elaborates on his own concept of conscience as follows:

> What the heart is to the body with its many functions,
> conscience is to the moral nature of man. It supplies

---

[14]C. E. de M. Sajous, Strength of Religion as Shown by Science (Philadelphia: F. A. Davis Co., 1914), p. 221.

[15]A. D. Foster, The New Dimensions of Religion (New York: The MacMillan Co., 1931), p. 176.

vitality to human nature and points out what Professor Hocking calls its cosmic direction. It literally sifts out the impurities in man's moral blood and sends fresh supplies to the extremities. Conscience thus conceived, like a wise commander, solidifies the gains, interprets the losses, furnishes plans of advance, and gives incentive to further victorious fighting. Its only authority is the authority of a vital organ, whose existence is always proof of cosmic origin and function. Conscience in the moral organism of man is as much a biological organ as are any of his bodily organs. Like the latter, man's conscience has grown up amid his moral tissues as a testimony to his experience and as a distinct response to his environment. It has therefore all the authority that reality can confer.[16]

Anderson[17] stresses the intuitive sense of conscience and states that this remains the highest tribunal for the evaluation of actions, thoughts and feelings. In his view the conscience can be considered to be the expression of the soul toward the supernatural law written on the heart.

Niebuhr[18] discusses the prevalent belief, exemplified in the writings of Saint-Simon and Auguste Comte, that human nature is guaranteed by the rational preferences for the benevolent as against egoistic impulses. The fallacies inherent in this position are pointed out at some length by Niebuhr who also discusses at length the concept of imago dei. While not clearly stating the relationship of this concept to that conscience, he indicates that the image of God in man is directly related to man's capacity for indeterminate self-transcendence. This appears to be closely related to the concept of conscience as being a vestigial remnant of God's consciousness toward evil.

---

[16]Ibid., p. 177.

[17]F. Anderson, Die Seele un das Gewissen (Leipzig, Germany: Felix Meiner Verlag, 1929), p. 54.

[18]R. Niebuhr, The Nature and Destiny of Man (New York: Charles Scribner's Sons, 1955), p. 150.

Stuart, with an overtly Darwinian orientation, has tried to trace the origin of conscience along similar phylogenetic pathways. She asks, for examples, "How did new evolutionary processes begin?" She continues:

> It seems today almost fantastic to imagine that there ever was at any time an inborn knowledge of an absolute good which a man was capable of seeing and free to disobey. But there was something very strong and absolute - the need to be loved and approved, by the family first, and then by the group. Good in any family or in any group was such conduct as was convenient to, and approved by, that family and that group. Evil in any family and any group was that which was inconvenient to, and disapproved by, that family and that group. There was not, in the early days at least, even any suggestion of a community of goods and evils, arrived at independently by many different human groups owing to some "inner light." The only "inner light" was the flickering dawn of love, and the good of some groups was the evil of others. It was only much later that a few wise men began to visualize forms of conduct which might be universally good, happy and free. But those were men who had outgrown both the childhood of the race, and the psychological childhood which has beset it for so long. In the beginning, goodness was approvedness, loveworthiness, evil disapprovedness, unloveworthiness - no more and no less.[19]

When speaking of the origin of the sense of evil she stresses the need for love and approval experienced in the primitive group:

> One might summarize the argument so far by suggesting four main sources of this sense of something wrong; the group, oneself, ignorance, and the magnitude of the human task. It was clear, because one felt it deeply within oneself, that one needed love and approval. One did something that the group disliked. Therefore that which one did was evil. The group indicated this to one. Moreover one felt it oneself. If it alienated the liking of the group it must be wrong.[20]

---

[19]G. Stuart, Conscience and Reason (London: George Allen and Unwin, Ltd., 1951), p. 162.

[20]Ibid., p. 46.

For Stuart the conscience was not originally the voice of God, but only came to be recognized as such because of sociological determinants, and because it represented the most god-like and omnipotent beings an individual will ever know, namely his parents.

Cohu also has a Darwinian orientation but tries to correlate this with Biblical revelation. Speaking of conscience, he asks:

> The question now before us is this: whence come to us these ideals, this categorical imperative, this soul-hunger? Why does our conscience speak to us with such a commanding voice of authority? Why do we realize an inward joy when we identify ourselves with the line of character or action it maps out for us as our duty, while we are conscious of a pain and friction when we acquiesce in whatever runs counter to its dictates?[21]

In trying to find an answer to this question, he summarizes the views of the Naturalists, who refuse to see anything supernatural in man's moral sense and ideals. Similarly, he notes the Comtist view that conscience and all man's spiritual ideals are due to the animal instincts of self-preservation and reproduction.

Such explanations are however inadequate for Cohu, who writes:

> But if conscience springs from social utilitarian needs, how does it come about that at every stage of man's history conscience sits in judgment on and breaks the laws of society? If the sense of obligation springs from society itself, why does our sense of duty rise so infinitely above the social standard and refuse to be merged in it? Can a spring rise above its own source?

---

[21]J. R. Cohu, _Vital Problems of Religion_ (Edinburgh: T. & T. Clark, 1914), p. 199.

> Why is man at all times dissatisfied with the social and religious standard as it is, and its laws, and often best fulfill the law by breaking it? Why does our conscience applaud a Christ who does violence to existing social and religious laws, however time-honored and hallowed their sanctions, and sets them at nought in the interests of society and religion itself? Once more, why does conscience, refusing to be merged in the social consciousness, ever set up for itself an ideal society, a Kingdom of God, a society straining after that justice, truth and love which alone satisfy conscience-needs?[22]

Cohu has no doubt that a natural explanation is insufficient. Conscience, he feels, is the Voice of God in the heart. Its laws of right and goodness are every whit as true and eternal as the laws of mathematics. Even as the mind refuses to conceive of a time or place where the angles of a triangle are not equal to two right angles, so does it refuse to conceive of a time or set of circumstances when love or unselfishness could be wrong. The laws of right and goodness are authoritative and of universal application because they are God's own handwriting in our heart and in the cosmic process, as the law of their being. But this does not mean that the individual conscience never errs. It often does. Yet it is not the Light of the God-Reason within that is dim, it is the eye of the heart. One needs to develop, train and exercise the inner eye, just as the bodily eye. This can be done by a pure and loyal life which will focus its gaze on all that is true and good, and thus accustom it to the light. Similarly, sensuality and selfishness blur its vision so that all its values are distorted and wrong. Hence, the conscience is not God's Light that grows within the individual, it is his

---

[22]Ibid., p. 201.

own receptivity of it.

Rehwinkel[23] has summarized his views on conscience in Baker's Dictionary of Theology. He defines conscience as that faculty in man by which he distinguishes between the morally right and wrong, which urges him to do that which he recognizes to be right and restrains him from doing that which he recognizes to be wrong, which passes judgment on his acts and executes that judgment within his soul. He notes that Webster defines conscience as the sense or consciousness of right and wrong and that Kant speaks of it as a consciousness of a court within man's being or the categorical imperative. Rehwinkel quotes Romans 2:14-15 to show that conscience is innate and universal adding that it is not the product of environment, training, habit, race impression or education, though it is influenced by all these factors.

Review of the pertinent literature reveals that views on the nature and function of conscience are many and varied. At the one end of the spectrum there are those who feel that conscience is an innate and God-given endowment of man. This view is espoused principally by the theological and paratheological writers and by a few psychologists. At the other extreme lie the environmentalists who feel that the conscience is derived in its entirety from the milieu by conditioning or learning or some type of identification with and internalization of authority figures. Freud is perhaps the outstanding representative of this

---

[23]A. M. Rehwinkel, "Conscience," Baker's Dictionary of Theology (Grand Rapids: 1960), p. 136.

latter viewpoint.

Among the theological writers there is almost as much divergence of opinion. Some feel that the conscience is actually God's voice in the human soul while others produce evidence to demonstrate that this cannot be so. Some equate conscience with the Law of God written on the heart while others, and perhaps the better exegetes, point out that it could more accurately be considered as a divine but vestigial consciousness of that inward law.

Summary

1. The philosopher, the psychologist, the anthropologist and the historian all view conscience from different perspectives.

2. Modern Psychology has, on the whole, been reluctant to discuss the concept of conscience.

3. Mc Dougall argued against the notion of an innate conscience and stressed the importance of environmental conditioning.

4. Thorndike considered that conscience may possibly be an instinctive endowment.

5. Vaughan taught that conscience develops out of the matrix of social approval and disapproval.

6. Woodworth stressed the importance of identification in the formation of the conscience.

7. Carmichael stated that conscience is a prerequisite of character although not necessarily a guarantor of it.

8. Freud, more than any other psychologist, gave attention and serious consideration to a study of the conscience and its operations.

9. In contrast to the psychologists, theologists have generally given serious consideration to the concept of conscience.

10. Delitzsch has examined the Biblical concept of conscience in some detail.

11. Sajous was of the opinion that the conscience is the internal voice of the Divine Spirit and is possessed by every man.

12. Foster considers conscience to be "a new biological organ of man" which serves an integrator of man's instincts.

13. Anderson felt that the conscience was the expression of the soul toward the law written on the heart.

14. Niebuhr has discussed the close relationship between conscience and the Imago Dei.

15. Stuart has attempted to trace the origin of conscience along phylogenetic pathways.

16. Cohu, although professing a Darwinian orientation, is not satisfied with purely naturalistic explanations for conscience and feels that it is, rather, the voice of God in the heart.

17. Rehwinkel has defined conscience as that faculty in man by which he distinguishes between the morally right and wrong.

Chapter III

THE STRUCTURE OF THE PSYCHIC APPARATUS

Within the psychoanalytic frame of reference, personality is considered to have structural divisions or segments
which perform separate and specific functions. These parts
are not to be considered as concrete realities or self-acting
entities, but as groups of forces and functions which are
dynamically inter-related. The concept of personality structure
and of conscience which is examined in this study is that
proposed by Freud who postulated three psychic segments in the
structure of the personality.[1] As will be seen many of the terms
used in describing these dynamic interrelationships are highly
metaphorical and figurative.

The id

In Freudian theory, the id is a collective name for the
primitive biological impulses and for that part of the personality
which harbors the unconscious instinctive desires and strivings
of the individual.[2] It represents the innate portion of the
personality which contains the driving psychic energy of personality functioning. The physiologically determined drives for
self-preservation such as for air, food, maintenance of bodily

---

[1]Sigmund Freud, The Ego and the Id, Standard Edition,
XIX (London: Hogarth Press, 1957).

[2]A Psychiatric Glossary, Committee on Public Information
of the American Psychiatric Association (Washington D. C., 1964),
p. 38.

temperature, physical integrity and procreation are considered
to be "id" functions. "Fight and flight" reactions and sexual
responses are thought of a "id" drives and affects. In cases
of psychopathology, where ego impairment exists, "id" impulses
may erupt into consciousness either in overt or derivative form.
The ego

In 1923, Freud[3] introduced the concept of the ego as a
coherent organization of mental processes which arises from
identifications with abandoned objects.

> The ego represents the sum of certain mental
> mechanisms, such as perception and memory and specific
> defensive mechanisms. The ego serves to mediate between
> the demands of primitive instinctual drives (the id),
> of the internalized parental and social prohibitions
> (the superego), and of reality. The compromises between
> these forces achieved by the ego tend to resolve intra-
> psychic conflict and serve an adaptive and executive
> function.[4]

The ego has neutral energies at its disposal and can transform
the energies of the id for its own use. In 1926 Freud described
the ego as autonomously initiating defense at the signal of
anxiety. In this manner, external reality was brought into the
picture along with the reality principle and secondary process.
This laid the ground work for the eventual development of the
theories of object relationships and adaptation to reality, i.e.
ego psychology.[5]

---

[3]Sigmund Freud, op. cit.

[4]A Psychiatric Glossary, p. 28.

[5]Sigmund Freud, The Problem of Anxiety (New York: Norton
Co., 1936), p. 125.

The ego, or reality-testing self, is thus that part
or function of the personality which establishes a relationship
with the external world. The ego, of course, is a group of
functions for which a metaphor is employed for ease of conceptualization. The ego deals with the environment, conscious
perception, thought, feeling and action, and is therefore the
consciously controlling portion of the personality. It contains
the evaluating, judging, compromising, solution-forming and
defense-creating aspects of the personality. The ego organization is concerned with such important functions as perception,
memory, evaluating and testing of reality, synthesizing of
experience and of acting as intermediary between the inner and
outer worlds and may be regarded as the integrative or executive
agency of the personality. The ego develops by a gradual learning
process and is determined largely by the individual's interactional
processes occurring between himself and others. Its functions
are to deal rationally with the requirements of reality, to adapt
behavior to the environment and other reality situations, and to
maintain harmony between the urges of the id and the demands and
aspirations of the superego.

For normal development and functioning of the personality,
the ego must be able to modify both the id drives and the superego's demands for acceptable conduct without extreme sacrifice
either of satisfaction of emotional and instinctive needs or of
ethical ideals. In this way, the ego serves as a mediator and
directs behavior into acceptable compromises between the blind

drives of the id and the inhibitions of the superego. The
guiding role of the id is that of the "pleasure principle,"
but that of the ego is the "reality principle," i.e., the demands
of the external world to which practical adaptation must be
made.

The ego directs instinctual energy into channels which
will, in the long run, bring the maximum pleasure and satisfaction. Its processes take place largely, but not entirely,
at the conscious level. It constructively integrates impulses
and thus secures mastery over them. If, through conscious
control, it deals effectively with inner and outer stresses, and
through reason it deals rationally with the requirements of
reality and of society, the ego is said to be "strong and healthy."

A "strong ego" achieves an integration of the demands
of the id, the superego and reality. It modifies or sublimates
primitive urges into socially acceptable patterns. The individual with a "strong ego" shows flexibility in handling the
various stresses of life without resorting to the inflexible and
repetitive defenses, which distinguish neurotic or psychotic
symptoms, or to characterological defects. If the ego is "weak"
and dominated by unconscious factors, it may undergo disinte-
grative processes. It may be unable to withstand the strain of
continued repression with the result that mental symptoms or
characterological defects appear.

The superego

The third hypothetical segment of the personality

structure and that segment which is the principal concern in
this study, because of its psychotheological significance, is
the "superego" or inhibiting and conscience-including component
of the personality. The superego functions to sustain the
internalized moral and social values. It is a conceptualized
advisor, admonisher and threatener, with both conscious and
unconscious aspects. The basic process of organization of this
function of the personality is advanced by the age of five, but
it continues to develop through adolescence and probably through
the young adult years. During the period of development, figures
of authority capable of punishing or rewarding become incorporated
into the personality, to form the distinguishable part known as
the "superego."

It is derived particularly from identification with
parents and their substitutes. The prohibitions and obligations
noted in these identifications are internalized and incorporated
into the unconscious psychological structure of the child.
Later the injunctions and prohibitions of other authorities and
of cultural influences are absorbed into the superego, the
whole acting as censor. The ascetic and moral demands of one's
social group become introjected and organized into an uncompro-
mising, unconscious, internal inhibitory law, of which the
superego is the personification. It acts as the supervisor of
the ego and of inner unconscious tendencies, and therefore as
the repressing part of the personality. It criticizes the ego
and causes pain to it whenever the latter tends to accept impulses

from the repressed part of the id. The superego may contain
irrational and even sadistic elements. It may threaten and
punish and thereby seek to maintain its authority. It does this
by creating anxiety and by producing guilt and remorse. If
the superego is severe and inflexible, the resulting fear will
lead to a rigid, inhibited, unhappy, anxious and often neurotic
personality.

Mention should also be made of the psychoanalytic notion
of psychic energy and how it developed. Freud began his career
as a research neurologist and during the most formative years
of his intellectual development, twenty to twenty-six, he was
an unpaid graduate assistant in the physiological institute
of the University of Vienna. The institute at that time was
dominated by the towering figure of Ernst Brucke, the colleague
and supporter of Helmholtz, who, in turn, was a disciple of
Johannes Muller, who is considered to be the greatest physiol-
ogist of the first third of the twentieth century. Helmholtz
was the father of the principle of the conservation of energy
and had attempted to show that the physical energies in the
external world influenced human sensory and perceptual function,
so that these functions themselves obeyed the laws of the trans-
formation and conservation of energy. Therefore, to those
students of human psychological functioning, who were loyal
to the tradition of Helmholtz and Brucke, the processes of
perception and motivation were viewed as following the same
laws of energy as events in the physical world. It follows

that when Freud formulated his theories of human psychological functioning, "perception, motivation, pleasure, pain, awareness, etc.," he naturally believed that there were neural energies corresponding to those processes and forming their objective and qualitative basis.

It was ideas, such as these, which led Freud in the 1890's to develop "A Project for a Scientific Psychology," in which he set forth a theory of human motivation in strictly neurological categories. What he was to call later "The Pleasure Principle" he called in the Project "The Principle of Neuronic Inertia." What he later called "The Reality Principle" and later still "The Ego," he called "An Organization of Impermeable Neurons" which had the effect of storing energy and inhibiting its release, rather than simply discharging it. To his great disappointment he was unable to develop his theory consistently and was forced to abandon the idea of a precise neurological referent for every psychological function. He did, however, retain the belief that the psyche functioned in a manner analogous to a physical energy system, in which energy was conserved, expended, diverted or directly discharged, inhibited in its expression, exaggerated in its expression, etc. This he referred to as an economic system of personality functioning. It would have been better, perhaps, if he had termed the system psycho-hydraulic as this would have been a more precise analogy. Thus, the Freudian concept of libido is the basic energy of the motivational life and is closely linked to sexual energy and drive.

In summary, the superego is that part of the personality associated with ethics, standards and self-criticism. It is formed by the infant's identification with important and esteemed persons in his early life, particularly parents. The supposed or actual wishes of these significant persons are taken over as part of the child's own personal standards to help form the conscience. In later life, they may become anachronistic and self-punitive, especially in psychoneurotic persons.[6]

A closely related aspect of the superego function, which will be examined in further detail, is that of the ego ideal, the internalized picture of what one desires to become, the idealized image toward which the ego strives. Thus the superego pushes toward the aspirations sustained in the ego ideal of the individual. Such ideals are gained through the identifications imposed by the growing child's contact with parents, teachers and others significant to him in both elder and peer groups.

Finally, whatever one may think of Freud's Project for a Scientific Psychology, "neuronic inertia," "permeable neurons" etc., these still remain the fundamental phenomenological givens, such as the patterning of biological drives through social conditioning and indoctrination, and these remain the same. Freud gave up his neurological mythology in favor of a more psychological theory in which the concept of psychic energy and the energy analogy was to remain an important part. The same concept of

---

[6]A Psychiatric Glossary, p. 73.

energy, even while remaining an analogy, will be of great use as we continue to examine the points of contact of psychological and theological thinking and in particular the psychotheology of spirit.

Summary

1. The id is a collective name for the primitive biological impulses or drives as well as the source of psychic energy for personality functioning.

2. The ego is the executive of the personality mediating between conscious and unconscious process.

3. The ego directs instinctual energy into channels which will, in the long run, bring narcissism pleasure and satisfaction.

4. A "strong ego" achieves an integration of the demands of the id, the Superego and reality.

5. The Superego is the conscience including segment of the personality and functions to sustain internalized moral and social values.

6. The Superego is derived particularly from identification with parents and their substitutes.

7. The psychoanalytic concept of psychic energy is an analogy and reflects Freud's early neurophysiologic training.

8. The Ego ideal is closely related to the Superego and is the idealized picture of what one desires to become.

Chapter IV

THE DEVELOPMENT OF THE SUPEREGO

The early origins of the superego

The majority of analytic writers feel that an individual
is not born with a superego or with an ego, as he is with the
instinctual reservoir known as the id. Sandler[1] states that
the child in the earliest weeks of life constructs schemata,
organized frames of influence within his mind, which serve
the purpose of adaption. As has been described earlier, this
is ego development. The schemata, or mental models, at first
have to do with instinctual satisfaction and at that time no
distinction is made between the inner and outer worlds. Gradually,
however, this distinction is made as the ego continues to
mature. Sandler speaks of an organizing activity and feels
that mental models must be constructed before internalization
and introjection can appear. These first models are primitive
and are under the dominance of the pleasure principle. Organizing activity includes the development of ego functions and
secondary process thinking. The development of the superego,
which will follow later, is dependent on this early development
of the ego.

----

[1]J. Sandler, "On the Concept of Super Ego" The Psychoanalytic Study of the Child, Vol. XV (New York: International Universities Press, 1960).

As the child begins to find his oneness with his mother, that is, his narcissistic union with her threatened, he feels anxiety and thus has impetus to restore the pleasurable state. He attempts to do this by using techniques of obedience and identification. These mechanisms will be discussed in detail later, since they are basic to the whole classic analytic concept of the development of the superego. The child, Sandler goes on to point out, feels one with and close to the object and regains the earlier feeling of happiness he had lost.

As a result of the conflicts engendered in this early period of development, there is first an attempt to deal with the realistic situation by denying or avoiding it, or by minimizing the unpleasant consequences. However, if development is to proceed and if the child is to be acceptable to his family and to the social group in which he and they live, he must more and more conform to and accept reality as defined by the personal and socially determined standards of the parents. In the accomplishment of this acceptance, a new organization of the mental apparatus, the superego, evolves or differentiates from the ego. The superego is considered to have its beginnings in the oral phase, when the baby is totally dependent on the mother and when the mother functions for the baby's as yet undeveloped ego. In the course of assimilating the external world, the child not only learns what gives him pleasure or pain, but also what gives the mother pleasure or pain. These experiences form guides to behavior but also provide grounds for internal conflict.

Little by little, the images of the mother and later of the
father build up within the child as guiding and controlling
influences, which direct the activity and impulses of the child,
in conformity with the parents' demands and needs, even when
the parents are not physically present. At first the child
may curb its activities only in response to a direct threat,
or a punishment by the parents, or he may respond to the parents'
unconscious expression of discomfort, when he does something
disapproved of by the parents' superego. The threat of punishment or the disapproving expression of the parents need not be
repeated, but the child responds as if it had been. In brief,
what was once an external influence, now is beginning to become
an internal influence.

Basic mechanisms

The basic mechanisms, according to classic psychoanalytic
theory,[2] utilized in the development of the superego, are
incorporation, introjection and identification.[3]

One of the problems in the area of understanding superego
development is the terminology. Hartman[4] states that incorporation

---

[2]E. Bergler, The Super Ego (New York: Grune and Stratton,
1952), p. 7.

[3]J. Lampl-de-Groot, The Development of the Mind (New
York: International Universities Press, 1965), pp. 114-125.

[4]H. Hartman and R. M. Loewenstein, "Notes on the Super
Ego" The Psychoanalytic Study of the Child, Vol. XVII, (New
York: International Universities Press, 1962).

is an instinctual activity belonging to the oral phase of development. Introjection, Hartman states, has been used synonymously with identification, incorporation and internalization. Some writers, however, prefer to use introjection to mean the process whereby identifications occur.

Introjection is closely related to the earlier pleasurable sensation associated with taking food in and incorporating other things into the body. Because this incorporation not only affords the body pleasure, but at the same time destroys the identity of the external object, the person may later rid himself of hostile impulses or symbolically eliminate a feared person by incorporating certain qualities of the feared person into the personality. This identification with other persons is commonly seen and undoubtedly plays a role in the child's attempt to imitate the father during and after the period of the oedipal conflict and castration anxiety. The adage, "If you can't lick them, join them," is an example of introjection.

The term introjection is used in analytic theory for defense mechanisms which allow the patient to avoid consciousness of an external frustration and its consequences. By attributing the act of rejection to himself, the aggression mobilized by the external frustration is not discharged against the external object, but against the self. Some analysts,[5] in addition, use the term introjection not only for an unconscious defense mechanism,

---

[5]H. P. Laughlin, Mental Mechanisms (Washington D. C.: Butterworths, 1963), pp. 1-26.

but also for that type of conscious identification which the child uses in order to establish a reinforced superego. When introjection is used as the term for an unconscious defense mechanism, it is assumed that this introjection allows a partial unconscious discharge of instinct tension and protects the individual from realization of his lack of power over the object.[6]

The superego in the genital phase.

The main development of the superego as a separate institution in the mental apparatus, takes place at the time of the developing oedipus complex. As the child must more and more conform to reality, he must also give up dependence on such unrealistic ego devices as denial, by which that which is unacceptable and disagreeable in the environment is dealt with as if it did not exist. As the oedipal situation develops and seeks solution, the analytic position is that then the superego really begins to develop. Freud felt that the superego developed as a precipitate within the ego and is correlated with a partial and relative reduction of interest in and dependence upon the real parents. The major source of self-esteem is no longer the parents, but now resides in the superego itself. Introjection has now occurred. Jacobson[7] states that the self-representation

---

[6]L. Eidelberg, A Comparative Pathology of the Neuroses (New York: International Universities Press, 1954), pp. 99-102.

[7]E. Jacobson, The Self and The Object World (New York: International Universities Press, 1954).

has been modified thusly and exists now as an internal agency.
At this point, behavior commensurate with the introjected
parental superego will cause a feeling of well-being and pride.
This is based on the feeling of returning to the original
narcissistic state. Behavior in an oppostie direction will
produce a feeling of guilt which in the young child, was originally
experienced as anxiety.

Another point which is not particularly stressed in the
literature is the loving aspect of the superego. By the process
of introjection of the parental superego, there is a reduction
of libidinal cathexis and a shift of cathexis now occurs to the
superego. In this way, the child can still hold on to his
parents and continue to feel their protection and loving care.
At this stage, the intensity of the superego depends on the child's
own aggressive and sadistic impulses, which are projected on
to the parents. It is this model which is introjected. It
does appear that the superego develops with the passing of the
oedipal conflict and is defensive in nature. It is defensive
in that, as libidinal cathexis is withdrawn from the parental
objects, the cathexis of the introjected object occurs. Aggressive
energy is thus liberated, and in order to protect the organism,
this energy is then directed into the superego.

The superego, according to Freud, is the heir of the
oedipus complex. The boy gives up his sensual desires for the
mother and hostile wishes toward the father, because of castration

fear. In Freud's words[8] the complex is "smashed to pieces by the shock of treatened castration." The girl renounces her oedipus complex more gradually and less completely as a result of fear over loss of the mother's love. Thus object choices are regressively replaced by identifications. "Object choice" refers to the desire to possess the individual sexually, whereas "identification" implies wanting to be like someone.

The frustrations of the oedipus complex are said to cause a regression from more differentiated types of object relationships to introjections and orality and to a point where sexual longing for an object is replaced by a sexual alternation within the ego. The introjected parents do not fuse with the rest of the ego because of the feeling of distance between parents and child. Instead, they combine with the previously existing parental introjects or superego forefunners to form a precipitate within the ego. These later identifications differ from the forerunners in the following way: the child, in order to escape conflicts revolving about love, guilt and anxiety, does not identify with the parents as they are, but with the idealized parents. He purifies their conduct in his mind, and the identification proceeds as if they were consistently true to the principles they explicitly profess or aspire to observe.

According to Freud the child thus identifies with the

---

[8]S. Freud, The Ego and The Id, Standard Edition, Vol. XIX, (London: Hogarth Press, 1957), p. 87.

superego of his parents.   Idealization was present earlier
in terms of attributing magical powers to the parents, but now
for the first time, the idealization concerns moral behavior.

Fenichel[9] admits that there are many unsolved problems
relating to the formation of the superego. If the superego
were simply an identification with the frustrating object of
the oedipus complex, then one would expect that the boy would
develop a motherly superego and the girl a fatherly one. Although
everyone does bear features of both parents in his superego,
this is not the outcome. Under our cultural conditions, says
Fenichel, the fatherly superego is generally decisive for both
sexes. The outstanding identification takes place with that
parent who is regarded as the source of decisive frustration,
usually the father, in the case of boys and girls alike.

Fenichel's statement, however, that the fatherly superego
is generally decisive for both sexes, is contradicted by data
obtained in the Blacky Pictures Research. Male college students
did tend to attribute fatherly characteristics to the superego,
but females, for the most part, described motherly ones.
Perhaps this departure from Fenichel's opinion may be a reflection
of the increasing influence of the mother in American life,
in contrast to the patriarchal European society in which psychoanalysis grew up. The related theoretical observation that the
superego in both sexes contains mixed parental elements was

---

[9]O. Fenichel, Psychoanalytic Theory of the Neuroses
(New York: W. W. Norton, 1945).

indirectly supported by the fact that there were 31 percent of the males who did present motherly superegos and 29 percent of the females, fatherly superegos.[10]

Freud referred to the superego as the representative of the id, referring to superego identification as the sublimation of oedipal strivings. These identifications are the result of early separation anxiety, aroused by threatened separation from the beloved mother. They continue to provide oedipal gratification even though desexualized. The motivating force behind these identifications and the intensifying of earlier identifications is castration anxiety which becomes transformed into fear of the superego. The fear of the loss of the love object and of loss of love is mastered by renouncing instinctual aims and by living with the internalized authority. As a substitute, the ego gains narcissistic gratification from the ego ideal and this will be discussed shortly. Freud regarded such substitution as an important part of character development. Thus the instinctual drives find two pathways through the ego for expression, i.e., directly if the drives are ego syntonic and indirectly through the superego.

At this stage, identification is of prime importance, because it is by this process whereby the child consciously and unconsciously emulates and tries to be like the parents, whom

---

[10]G. S. Blum, "A Study of the Psychoanalytic Theory of Psychosexual Development," Genetic Psychological Monographs (New York: International Universities Press, 39: 3-99, 1952).

he both loves and fears. Identification acknowledges, at least
to some extent, the reality of the discrepancy in size and
ability and hence serves both as an impetus toward development
and as a means of defense against the unacceptable hostile feeling
toward the rival parent. When identification is successfully
accomplished, many of the characteristics of the loved and feared
object actually become an integral part of the self. With this,
the boy, for example, is able to gradually give up the idea of
displacing his father and becomes willing to wait and work to
be like him. Now the boy may enter a phase of admiration and
even hero worship for the father. Overt hostility toward his
father (or mother) may now even be replaced by greater affection.
Through a process of internalization of the characteristics and
standards of the parents, the child is establishing an internal
system concerned with expectations of both punishment and reward.
In addition, the superego is made up of the internalized repre-
sentations of all "the dos and don'ts" of the parents (and later
teachers, guides, etc.) and through them, representatives of the
mores and the moral code of the culture. Thus there also develops
an internal agency for rewarding and punishing. When one does
what he conceives as being wrong, something to be disapproved of,
one feels guilt and with it a feeling of worthlessness and a need
for punishment and atonement. This leads logically to the concept
of social conscience.

The superego in the latency phase

In latency, with the resolution of the castration complex,

a process of integration and refinement takes place, resulting
in the deepening in the psychic structure of more specific
attitudes and character traits. Hartman, Kris and Loewenstein[11]
discuss the changes which take place in the superego during
latency. At first, the newly formed superego is exposed to
many conflicting demands; it tends to be overly rigid and rather
than compromise, it yields. Early in latency, obsessional
symptoms are said to be very frequent. As the phase progresses,
there is a gradual adjustment in superego functions and this is
due partly to the growth of intellectual comprehension and
educational or religious indoctrination, but it is also partly
due to the fact that the function of the superego is less in
danger and therefore needs less protection.

Similarly, Bornstein[12] suggests that there are really
two major phases in the latency period, the first from 5-1/2
and 8 years, and the second from 8 until about 10 years. The
element common to both is the strictness of the superego in its
evaluation of incestuous wishes. The ego in the earlier phase,
still buffeted by impulses, is threatened by a new and foreign
superego, which continues in a harsh and rigid manner. Later,
however, the ego is exposed to less severe conflicts as a result
of diminished sexual demands and a more pliable superego. The

[11]H. Hartman, and E. Kris, "Comments on the Formation
of Psychic Structure," The Psychoanalytic Study of the Child,
Vol. II, (New York: International Universities Press, 1948).

[12]B. Bornstein, "On Latency," The Psychoanalytic Study
of the Child, Vol. VI, (New York: International Universities
Press, 1951).

organism then devotes greater attention to coping with reality.

The superego in adolescence

With the advent of pre-adolescence, the balanced relationship or truce between the ego and the id in latency is disrupted.
Physiological forces stimulate the instinctual processes and
upset the balance. The ego, already strengthened and consolidated,
struggles desperately to regain the equilibrium by using all the
defenses in its repertory. This conflict is frequently translated
readily into behavior. While the id is winning, there is an
increase in fantasy, lapses into pre-genital sexual gratification
and aggressive or even criminal actions. While the ego is ahead,
there are various forms of anxiety, neurotic symptoms and inhibitions. The ego also alienates itself from the superego during
adolescence.[13] Since the superego is still intimately related
to the parents, it is itself treated as a suspicious, incestuous
object. The principal effect of this break between ego and
superego is to increase the danger which threatens from the
instincts. Since the former alliance of superego and ego is at
an end, the defensive measures prompted by superego anxiety become
inoperative, and the ego falls back to the level of pure, instinctual anxiety, accompanied by primitive protective measures.

With the onset of adolescence, the individual is subjected
to a resurgence and recrudescence of the instinctual drives. The
drives are now on a more mature genital level and the aim shifts

---

[13]G. Engel, Psychological Development in Health and
Disease (London: W. B. Saunders Co., 1962), pp. 141-154.

from the parents to a substitute object in the environment. The
ego is stronger, and has better defenses for coping with these
drives, even though there is a separation from the parents and
loss of support from the parents' egos. The individual has to
face his instinctual drives and the demands of the outer world
more and more on his own. In facing this task, he comes to rely
more not only on his superego but also on his ego ideal, which
begins to lose some of its magical qualities and idealizations.

The superego becomes internalized as the real parents'
demands become less important. This means that he also gives
up the parents as love objects. The young child obeys the parents'
demands to obtain love and avoid punishment. This renunciation
is a long and difficult process, and as the secondary autonomous
functions develop, the superego gives up part of its infantile
identifications. Edith Jacobson[14] points out the contradiction
arising "between the adolescent's need to copy with the loss of
his infantile love objects by fortifying his identification with
them, and the fact that these very identifications become more
and more dispensable." The superego must lift its barriers
enough to permit mature object relationships. This must be
accomplished without depletion of secondary narcissism and loss
of self-esteem.

---

[14]E. Jacobson, "The Self and the Object World,"
Psychoanalytic Study of the Child, Vol. IX, (New York: International Universities Press, 1964).

Goals which were unacceptable during the preoedipal
and oedipal periods now become acceptable, only the objects are
changed. This means more mature and reality-tested identifications in the superego, with the parents and others as normal,
healthy, sexually active individuals. However, a certain amount
of magical thinking permits a degree of idealization, which
remains in the ego ideal. Some of this remains in the adult
and may spread to other objects in the environment, such as
teachers, heroes, public figures and the truer love objects.
This requires and results in an increase in the ego's ability to
test reality and in better and more mature ego defenses. The
adolescent must be understood in terms of searching and change.[15]
From the onset of puberty until beginning adulthood, there is
constant vacillation, regression and progression within the
ego/superego structure, until there takes place a final reintegra-
tion within the psychic organization on the adult level.[16] This
process leads to the formation of what Jacobson calls a
"weltanschauung" within the individual. This means a certain way
of viewing the world and our place in it. This "weltanschauung"
includes ideals, ethics, moral principles and opinions on sexual,
racial, national, religious and political problems. Some of

---

[15]A. Freud, "Adolescence," in The Psychoanalytic Study
of the Child, Vol. XIII, (New York: International Universities
Press, 1958).

[16]I. M. Josselyn, The Adolescent and His World, (New York:
Family Service Association of American, 1952).

these are a result of identification with objects, and some, because of rebellion and the giving up of such identifications in the light of reality experiences. This results in the adolescent being in a constant state of vacillation and shifting series of attitudes and opinions, until more or less permanent attitudes and opinions are reached. In the adult, such shifting is more reality-tested, and less searching in nature. Both the superego and the ego ideal are torn down and there is a simultaneous growth in ego capacity. These growing up problems of the adolescent are connected with feelings of "guilt" and "shame." These affects and their origin will be discussed in a later section.

Later modifications of the superego

Even though the superego has, so to speak, come into being with the passing of the oedipal conflict, further modifications occur during later life, and as has been described, numerous vacillations occur during the phase of adolescence. Just how long such further modifications may occur is debatable. Hartman[17] states, however, that further superego identifications probably do not occur often, but may. Thus new ego identifications may occur, and thus the superego may be modified. This allows for reduction of tension between the superego and the ego.

Relationships between the superego, ego and id

The superego and ego are related to each other in that both are based on the external world. The superego is a sort of

---

[17]H. Hartman and R. M. Loewenstein, "Notes on the Superego," in Psychoanalytic Study of the Child, Vol. XVII, (New York: International Universities Press, 1962).

a second ego with a more limited sphere of functioning. Since
the incorporation of the external world in the superego occurs
relatively late, the superego remains closest to the outside
world. To support this statement, Fenichel[18] says that many
persons remain uninfluenced in their behavior and self-esteem,
not only by what they consider correct themselves, but also by
the consideration of what others may think. Superego and objects
that make demands are not always clearly distinguished. Superego
functions may also be easily reprojected, that is displaced onto
newly appearing authority figures. Another factor which supports
the belief that the construction of the ego is the role played
by auditory stimuli. For the ego, auditory stimuli or words
become important after the kinesthetic and visual experiences
of the archaic ego. For the superego, on the other hand, words
are more important at the very beginning of its formation, since
parental attitudes are mainly incorporated by way of the ear.

The superego is also related to the id through its genesis.
The most essential objects of the id, the objects of the oedipus
complex, live on in the superego. This genesis is said to explain
the urgent, instinct-like, irrational character of many superego
strivings, which in normal development must be overcome by
reasonable judgment of the ego. In Freud's words, "the superego
dips deeply into the id."

Even though certain writers speak of the ego, superego

---

[18]O. Fenichel, The Psychoanalytic Theory of Neurosis
(New York: W. W. Norton, 1945), p. 186.

and ego ideal as specific separate structures, such artificial
differentiation may lead to difficulties in understanding clinical
material. It is preferable to subsume all three under the name
"ego" and see the superego and ego ideal as certain functions
aiding the ego to perform its task of mastery over instinctual
drives and environmental stimuli, and in the process of identification. These functions can be thought of as developing as
the result of the ego's interactivity with the id and environment;
in other words, in the organization of defense.

Functions of the superego

Freud[19] gave a summary of the functions of the superego.
He said:

> The torments caused by the reproaches of conscience
> correspond precisely to a child's dread of losing his
> parents' love, a dread which is replaced in him by the
> moral agency. On the other hand, if the ego has suc-
> cessfully resisted a temptation to do something that
> would be objectionable to the superego, it feels its
> self-respect raised and its pride increased, as though
> it had made some previous acquisition. In this way,
> the superego continues to act the role of an external
> world to the ego, although it has become part of the
> internal world. During the whole of a man's later
> life, it represents the influence of his childhood, of
> the care and education given to him by his parents, of
> his dependence on them, of the childhood which is so
> greatly prolonged in human beings by a common family
> life. And in all of this, what is operating is not
> only the personal qualities of his parents, but also
> everything that produces a determining effect upon
> them themselves, the tastes and standards of the social
> class in which they live, and the characteristics and
> traditions of the race from which they spring.

The functions of the ego center around relationship to
reality. It holds an executive position--the aim being to

[19] S. Freud, _An Outline of Psychoanalysis_, Standard
Edition, (London: Hogarth Press, 1938), pp. 89-90.

effect some sort of compromise between pressures from the superego and the outside world. On the other hand, the functions of the superego center around moral demands.[20] Self-criticism and the formation of ideals are said to be the essential manifestations of the superego. It represents the incorporated standards of society, including parental attitudes as interpreted by the child, and the child's own ideals for himself. To a great extent, the superego is unconscious, since it was incorporated by the child very early and without awareness. The fact that it is largely unconscious and inaccessible for reality-testing accounts partially for its irrational harshness. With the establishment of the superego, various mental functions are altered: anxiety changes in part into guilt feelings. It is no longer an external danger, that is loss of love or castration, which is feared, but an inner representative of this danger, that is the "loss of the superego's protection." Such loss is felt as an extremely painful decrease in self-esteem. The privilege of granting or refusing the narcissistic supplies needed by the child to maintain his equilibrium is now taken over by the superego.

The superego is the heir of the parents, not only as a source of threats and punishment, but also as a source of protection and as a provider of reassuring love. Being on good or bad terms with one's superego becomes as important as being on good or bad terms with parents previously was. The change

[20]J. A. Arlow, and C. Brenner, Psychoanalytic Concepts and Structural Theory (New York: International Universities Press, 1964).

from parents to superego is a pre-requisite for the development
of independence.[21] Self-esteem is no longer regulated by
approval or rejection by external objects, but rather by the
feeling of having or not having done the right thing. Complying
with the superego's demands brings feelings of pleasure and
security of the same type that children experience from external
supplies of love. Refusing this compliance brings feelings of
guilt and remorse which are similar to the child's feelings of
not being loved any more.

Klein's views of the superego

As has been seen, orthodox psychoanalytic theory charac-
terizes the first year as witnessing the early tentative phases
in the formation of ego structure. The superego in classic
analytic theory is thought to be completely non-existent at this
time. Melanie Klein[22] the leader of the British school of
psycho-analysis, postulates the act of functioning of a well-
developed ego and superego in the first year of life. Klein's
system is predicated on the assumption of unconscious fantasies
which she inferred from her work in analyzing neurotic children.
These unconscious fantasies are said to be the primary content
of all mental processes and underline all conscious and unconscious
thoughts. In the first few months of life, Klein sees evidence

---

[21]A. Freud, Ego and Mechanisms of Defense (New York:
International Universities Press, 1946).

[22]M. Klein, The Psycho-analysis of Children (London:
Hogarth Press, 1949).

for a wide range of highly differentiated object relations, some libidinal and some aggressive. The infant at six months already loves, hates, desires, attacks and wishes to destroy and to dismember his mother. Being afraid of his destructive impulses. Numerous complications can follow, such as the possibility of spitting out or rejecting the superego.

Rank's views of the superego

Rank[23] considers the basis of the superego to be the mother-child relationship and its function is built up genetically from inhibited sadism. There are three different superegos, or three different stages in superego development:

1. The biological superego occurs very early in
   life. There is a missing of the breast and
   this arouses sadistic libido. This libido
   is partially drained in the form of rage
   reactions against the mother, but the rest
   is dammed up in the ego and leads to the formation of inner privations or inhibitions.

2. There is a moral superego, which arises at
   the anal stage as a result of toilet training
   and which provides content for the sado-
   masochistic mechanism.

3. There is a social superego, which comes into

---

[23]W. Healy, A. F. Bronner, A. M. Bowers, The Structure and Meaning of Psycho-analysis (New York: Knopf, 1940).

being in the oedipal period with identifications and the introjection of parental
prohibitions.

For Rank, the real nucleus of the superego is the "strict"
mother"--not the actual mother, but the mother as sadistically
conceived by the child. He distinguishes between a "primitive"
superego and a "correctly functioning" one. The primitive
superego shows up in a need for punishment in a constant attempt
to unload itself or to reestablish punishment from the outside.

Rank also differentiates the female and male superegos.
The girl at the oedipus period retains the primary biological
superego, whereas the boy builds up over the primary maternal
superego the paternal social superego. Thus the female superego
consists much more of inhibitions than guilt feelings, whereas
in the male, anxiety dominates.

Fromm's views of the superego

Fromm[24] conceives of an authoritarian and a humanistic
conscience. According to Fromm, the authoritarian conscience
corresponds to Freud's superego. It is the voice of an internalized external authority, such as the parents, and differs
from fear of punishment or hope of reward only in the sense that
it has been internalized. Whether the child behaves in a good
or a bad direction depends solely upon the goodness or badness
of his authority figures, and nothing more. The force of the

---

[24]E. Fromm, Man for Himself (New York: Rinehart, 1947).

authoritarian conscience is dependent on a continuing relationship with the external authority. If the external figures leave the scene, the conscience weakens and loses power. At the same time, the conscience influences the image which a person has of the external authorities, since there is a need to set up an ideal and to project affection upon the authorities. Very often, this interaction of internalization and projection results in an unmistakable conviction in the ideal character of the authority, a conviction which is immune to all contradictory and critical evidence.

The contents of the authoritarian conscience are derived from the commands and taboos of the authorities. It is rooted in the emotions of fear and of admiration for the authority. Good conscience is consciousness of pleasing the authority. On the other hand, guilty conscience is the consciousness of dis-pleasing it. The authoritarian conscience produces a feeling of well being and security for it implies approval by the authority. The guilty conscience produces fear and insecurity, because acting against the will of the authority imples the danger of being punished and deserted.

The humanistic conscience, on the other hand, is not the internalized voice of an authority, but rather the voice of the individual himself. It is a reaction of the total personality to its proper functioning or dysfunctioning--a knowledge within oneself of success or failure in the art of living. Humanistic conscience is the expression of man's self-interest and integrity.

Its goal is productiveness and happiness. Guilt feelings arise when the self goes unfulfilled and they express themselves typically in fears of disapproval or of death and old age. For example, if a person cannot approve of himself because he fails in the task of living productively, he has to substitute approval by others for approval of himself. Thus unconscious guilt feelings lead to fear of disapproval.

According to Fromm, everyone has both an authoritarian and a humanistic conscience. The relative strength of each as well as the relations between the two depend on the individual's experiences. One form of relationship is that in which guilt feelings are consciously felt in terms of the authoritarian conscience, while dynamically they are rooted in the humanistic conscience. A person may feel consciously guilty for not pleasing authorities, while unconsciously he feels guilty for not living up to his own expectations of himself. If the conscience is based upon rigid and unassailable irrational authority, the development of the humanistic conscience can be almost entirely suppressed. Usually, the authoritarian conscience exists as a pre-condition for the formation of humanistic conscience, but Fromm feels that this is not necessary in a non-authoritarian society.

Summary

1. Most authorities consider the Superego to be learned in character.

2. As a means of dealing with early conflicts the child tends to conform more and more to and accept reality as

defined by the parents.

3. The basic mechanisms, according to classic psycho-analytic theory, utilized in the development of the Superego, are incorporation, introjection and identification.

4. The main development of the Superego as a separate institution in the mental apparatus, takes place at the time of the developing oedipus complex.

5. In the formation of the Superego identification is of prime importance because it is by this process whereby the child consciously and unconsciously emulates his parents.

6. In the latency stage, continued adjustment in Superego functions occurs.

7. In adolescence, with the recrudesence of instinctual strivings, the Superego is treated as a suspicious object since it is so intimately associated with the parental figures.

8. Continued motification of the Superego continues all throughout life.

9. The functions of the Superego center around moral demands.

10. Melanie Klein, in contrast to classical psycho-analysts, postulates the existence of a functioning Superego in the first year of life.

11. Rank considered the basis of the Superego to be the mother-child relationship and its function to be related genetically to inhibited sadism.

12. Rank differentiates between a biological, moral and a social Superego.

13. Fromm's view is that both an authoritarian and a humanistic conscience exist in every individual.

Chapter V

THE SUPEREGO AND THE EGO IDEAL

In reviewing the literature, it appears that the first use of the term "ego ideal" was by Freud in 1914.[1] His initial concept of the "ego ideal" was that "the individual sets up an ideal for himself by which he measures his actual ego."

Freud, as well as many other theorists have used superego and ego ideal as synonymous terms, while at other times a distinction has been made between the two. In Freud's last works, he seems to de-emphasize any distinction or difference between the ego ideal and the superego, and rather emphasized that they were synonymous and could be considered as a structure of the ego. In 1923, Freud stated that "we should keep firmly to the fact that the separation of the ego from an observing, critical, punishing ego, must be taken into account."[2] Whether Freud's real beliefs were to consider the superego and ego ideal as synonymous, is open to debate.

Piers and Singer[3] in their monograph appear to have been cognizant of Freud's attempts, on one hand, to make the term

---

[1]S. Freud, On Narcissism, Standard Edition, (London: Hogarth Press, 1914).

[2]S. Freud, The Ego and the Id, Standard Edition, (London: Hogarth Press, 1923), p. 187.

[3]G. Piers, and M. Singer, Shame and Guilt (Springfield: Thomas Press, 1953).

55

ego ideal and superego synonymous, but on the other hand, even within the same paper, they have attempted at times to distinguish them. Piers[4] stated that "it seems immaterial whether one wishes to regard the ego ideal merely as one particular aspect of the superego, or as a psychological formation entirely separate and independent." However, from a study of his monograph, it appears that Piers in his own mind treated the ego ideal and superego as separate.

Piers describes the ego ideal as representing the sum of the positive identifications with parental images. Furthermore, the ego ideal contains strata, in that later identifications are made with others than the parents, and even though they may be superficial, they are important in that they determine one's social role in specific social situations. Both early and later identifications contain aspects of the loving, reassuring parents, who approved of the individual's measuring up to ideals. Piers also states that there is a variable amount of narcissistic omnipotence which shapes the ego ideal. If the core of narcissistic omnipotence is exaggerated, it could well result in a perfectionistic ego ideal, which would be impossible to attain and consequently generate tension between the ego and the ego ideal. Piers calls the tension generated by the disparity between the unconscious ego and unconscious ego ideal a shame which is manifested by anxiety. It is at this point that a

---

[4]Ibid., p. 190.

differentiation is made between failure to measure up to the unconscious ego ideal (shame) and transgression against the prohibitions of the unconscious superego (guilt). It is thought that the shame anxiety is based on fear of loss of love and at a deeper level, death by emotional starvation. It seems logical then, that the threat of loss of love comes from the loved parental images or the positive images. However, it should be noted that a loved image may be modified by the projection of the unconscious omnipotence of the individual onto the loved images and then internalized, or it can be channeled directly into the ego ideal. Guilt anxiety in most cases is equivalent to castration anxiety, and develops from the ego transgressing the prohibitions of the unconscious superego and fears of anni-hilation and mutilation as punishment under the talion principle.

In general, then, utilizing some of Piers' concepts, the ego ideal represents the positive goals internalized by an individual through identification with the goals of the parents, peer groups and key figures in early and in later life. These are in turn modified by the individual's own core of narcissistic omnipotence, which may be projected initially onto the parents and then internalized and/or channeled directly into the ego ideal. When the individual is in the act of successfully meas-uring up to this ego ideal, it would seen to be affectively experienced as "funktionlust" as described by Bubhler. Some theorists as Hendric, Fenichel, Alexander, Erickson and Straus, feel that behind the actual attaining of one's ideals is the "instinct of mastery" or maturation drive. To such writers, it appears that the ego rather than the id is the seat of the ability to master and achieve one's ego ideals. It is possible, however, that the source of the psychic energy which the ego utilizes to achieve mastery comes from the id, but this is an economic or "hydraulic" problem.

Jeanne Lampl-de-Groot[5] views the ego ideal as a structure entirely separate from the superego. She believes that the ego ideal exists as early as the first year of life when the infant makes no differentiation between the self and the object and is basically narcissistic. The ego ideal at this stage is represented as a hallucinatory wish fulfillment. Later when the infant has ego boundaries, when he can differentiate himself from the object, he has fantasies of his own grandeur and omnipotence. The infant becomes quite aware of his need for his parents and de Groot feels that the parents are then fantasied as being omnipotent, so he can share in their omnipotence to compensate for his lack of omnipotence, or powerlessness. De Groot concludes that the true formation of a realistic ego ideal comes only after the individual gives up the fantasied ideal parents.

De Groot's concept of the ego ideal and superego being considered separate, seems to be based on the differences in their development. Briefly, she sees the superego based initially

---

[5]J. Lampl-de-Groot, "Ego Ideal and Superego," in Psychoanalytic Study of the Child, Vol. XVII, (New York: International Universities Press, 1961).

on experiences and on pleasurable sensations. As a result,
there is a giving up of wish fulfillment and giving in to
parental demands to obtain their love. In the pre-oedipal phase,
de Groot states there is internalization of specific parental
demands by identification. Finally, the individual accepts the
restrictions, of not only his parents, but also of the environment in order to get along satisfactorily from a social standpoint, within the family, peer group or class structure.

In 1932, Nunberg,[6] as did de Groot, thought the ego
ideal and superego to be quite separate. One of his concepts
of the ego ideal was concerned with Freud's notion of shame in
the "Three Essays on Sexuality" (1905). Their shame was considered
to be a reaction formation against exhibitionism. As did de Groot,
he contrasts the ego ideal with the superego: "The ego submits
to the ego ideal out of love; the ego ideal is an image of the
loved object in the ego, whereas the ego submits to the superego
out of fear."[7] This differs somewhat from Piers' concepts, but
in other ways is rather similar.

Laufer[8] considers the ego ideal as part of the superego.

---

[6]H. Nunberg, "The Synthetic Function of the Ego" and
"The Feeling of Guilt," in The Practice and Theory of Psychoanalysis, Chapters VIII and IX, (New York: International Universities Press, 1948).

[7]Ibid., p. 172.

[8]M. Laufer, "Ego Ideal and Pseudo Ego Ideal in Adolescence,"
Psychoanalytic Study of the Child, Vol. XIS, (New York:
International Universities Press, 1964).

It contains attributes and models which the ego strives to attain as a means of recapturing the narcissistic perfection of childhood. It is his opinion that social adaptation depends on the amount of distortion of the idealized parent himself, but occurs in pre-oedipal and oedipal phases, and on how much becomes truly internalized.

Sandler, Meers and Holder[9] attempted to clarify Freud's views on the ego ideal. In his paper "On Narcissism" (1914), they thought his major emphasis was on the development of the ideal as being continuous with the original narcissistic state: "The subject's narcissism makes its appearance displaced onto the new ego ideal ego which like the infantile ego, finds itself possessed of every perfection that is of value ... what he projects before him as his ideal is the substitute for the lost narcissism of his childhood in which he was his own ideal." Freud also pointed out that impulses undergo repression, if they conflict with one's culture and ethical ideas. "Repression proceeds from the ego; we might say with greater precision that it proceeds from self-respect of the ego."[10] Freud, particularly in regarding the narcissistic aspect of the ego ideal, distinguished between the conscience and the ego ideal.

---

[9]J. Sandler, A. Holder, D. Meers, "The Ego Ideal and the Ideal Self," Psychoanalytic Study of the Child, Vol. XVIII, (New York: International Universities Press, 1963).

[10]S. Freud, On Narcissism, Standard Edition, (London: Hogarth Press, 1914), pp. 202-203.

Freud continued to hold the same position in the "Introductory Lectures" (1916-1917) saying that the ego ideal was
"created by man for himself" in the course of development, and
"for the purpose of recovering thereby the self-satisfaction
bound up with the primary infantile narcissism, which since
those days has suffered so may shocks and modifications."
Regarding the conscience still as a separate entity, he stated:
"We recognize in this self-criticizing faculty, the ego censorship."[11]

In "Group Psychology and Analysis of the Ego," Freud
saw in melancholia "the ego divided--fallen into two pieces,
one which rages against the second--the piece which behaves
so cruelly is not unknown to us. It comprises the conscience,
a critical agency within the ego which even in normal times takes
up a critical attitude toward the ego."[12] Freud here seemed
to include the conscience in the term ego ideal. In "The Ego
and the Id," (1923)[13] where he introduced the structural theory,
there is no distinction between the ego ideal and superego. If
anything, Freud seems to emphasize the critical, judgmental and
punitive aspects of the superego. In the "New Introductory

[11]S. Freud, Introductory Lectures, Standard Edition,
(London: Hogarth Press, 1917), p. 107.

[12]S. Freud, Group Psychology and the Analysis of the
Ego (London: Hogarth Press, 1922).

[13]S. Freud, The Ego and the id, Standard Edition,
(London: Hogarth Press, 1923).

Lectures" (1923),[14] he refers to the superego as the vehicle of the ego ideal. The superego then is the ideal parent. In summary, it seems that Freud at various times described the ego ideal as the conscience, observer, ideal self-image and ideal parental introjects.

Sandler[15] and his group consider what Freud, in "On Narcissism" (1914), calls the ego ideal as the ideal self. They suggest that the genesis of the ideal self is an identification with aspects of loved, admired or feared objects. The objects do not need to be present if introjected. Other identifications which seem to be dependent on the initial identifications are with the image of the "good" or "desirable" child, as conveyed by the object and with certain parts of the individual's wishes for an ideal state.

Sandler describes shame as "I cannot see myself as I want to see myself or as I want others to see me." This seems to differ little from Piers' and Singer's concept. However, Sandler's view on guilt differs considerably from that of Piers' and Singer's. "I do not really want to be what I feel I ought to be." It would thus seem that they are still speaking of shame and not of guilt.

---

[14]S. Freud, New Introductory Lectures, (New York: Norton, 1933).

[15]J. Sandler, "On the Concept of Superego," Psychoanalytic Study of the Child, Vol. XV, (New York: International Universities Press, 1960).

Joseph Sandler[16] and his group attempt to clarify and summarize Freud's use of the term ego ideal as follows:

1. In "On Narcissism" (1914) and in the "Introductory Lectures" (1916-1917) the term was used to refer to the individual's ideals for himself, as a result of his attempt to regain infantile narcissism. It is here distinguished from the conscience.

2. In "Group Psychology" (1921), the conscience was included in the term.

3. In 1923, it was used in the same sense as superego, i.e., a mental structure.

4. In 1932, the superego is referred to as "the vehicle of the ego ideal," the word ideal referring to the ideal parent as embodied in the superego.

Amy Reich distinguishes the superego as "a more reality syntonic structure." The ego ideal as "the earlier, more narcissistic one." She states that "the ego ideal expresses what one desires to be, the superego what one ought to be."[17]

Jeanne Lampl-de-Groot[18] sees the ego ideal as an agency of wish fulfillment formed by differentiation from the first months of life. Its content is "I am like my omnipotent parents."

---

[16]J. Sandler, "The Classification of Superego Material," Psychoanalytic Study of the Child, Vol. XVIII, (New York: International Universities Press, 1962).

[17]A. Reich, "Early Identifications and Superego," The International Journal of Psychoanalysis, 1954, 18: 76-89.

[18]J. Lampl-de-Groot, op. cit., pp. 94-108.

The superego is seen as an agency of restriction, which is matured only in latency, at the end of the oedipal phase. Its content is, "I will live up to the demands of my parents." In normal development, the superego and ego ideal guide the ego in its task of obtaining sufficient gratification and on the other sublimating and modifying part of them in order to live up to the demands of the outside world and cope with restrictions.

This material can be summarized by stating that the ego ideal and superego are sub-functions of the ego. They are differentiated out of the matrix of the ego by forces from the representational world of the child, of ideational and affective content, which the developing child constructs on the basis of experiences. Sandler points out how this world grows with object relationships and learning. For practical purposes, it is immaterial whether they are separate structures or one structure. The ego ideal is the more primitive structure and contains more archaic and magical elements than the superego. However, it is impossible to make always a clear cut separation in a meaningful way between the ego ideal and the superego, because there is of necessity some overlapping. With the beginning of differen- tiation and the experiencing of both gratification and unpleasure, the child begins to indulge in what Freud calls "hallucinatory wish fulfillment." This occurs during the narcissistic stage. With separation, there is the beginning of the ego ideal from two sources. Firstly, fantasies of omnipotence which counteract the fears of separation and heighten self-esteem. Freud in 1914 stated, "that which he projects ahead of him, as his ideal, is merely his substitute for the lost narcissism of his childhood, the time when he was his own ideal."[19] And secondly, his idealization and over-estimation of his parents, which is retained magically in the core of the ego ideal and is not reality tested.

This twin aspect of the ego ideal maintains the child's desire to remain one with the love object. Lampl-de-Groot states: "No mother, no matter how loving and devoted, can grant every wish or abolish every pain in her child. To deal with this, the child develops his hallucinatory wish fulfillment and his comforting fantasies of grandeur and omnipotence."[20]

Sandler[21] speaks of the ego ideal as existing long before the formation of the superego proper, and its content categorized as follows:

1. Identifications with aspects of loved, admired and feared objects. These objects may be introjects (often the formation of the superego proper) or may be at any time persons in the individual's environment.

2. Identification with the image of the "good" or "desirable" child as conveyed by the object.

[19]S. Freud, "On Narcissism" Standard Edition, (London: Hogarth Press, 1914), p. 106.

[20]J. Lampl-de-Groot, op. cit., pp. 94-108.

[21]J. Sandler, op. cit., pp. 128-148.

3. Identifications with previous shapes of the individual's own self. By this is meant the construction of the ideals based upon the wish to attain "ideal" states previously experienced in reality or in fantasy.

Freud stressed the role of the ego ideal as the heir to primary narcissism. Hartman and Lowenstein said that the ego ideal can be considered a rescue operation for narcissism. John M. Murray[22] points out how important this process is for the building up of self-esteem. "The ego ideal is transformed from narcissism by a change of aim and object relationships akin to sublimation of instinct, that is, an abstraction may replace a narcissistic hunger."

Jeanne Lampl-de-Groot[23] sees the superego and ego ideal as completely separate structures and differentiates the genesis of each. In summary, she sees the ego ideal as follows:

1. Hallucinatory wish fulfillment in the narcissistic stage in which self and outer world are not yet distinguishable.
2. Fantasies of grandeur and omnipotence of the self, after the infant has become aware of a distinction between self and objects.
3. Fantasies of the parents being omnipotent and sharing their omnipotence after experiencing

[22] J. M. Murray, "Narcissism and the Ego Ideal," *Journal of the American Psychoanalytic Association*, 1964, 37: 106-121.

[23] J. Lampl-de-Groot, op. cit., pp. 94-108.

his own powerlessness.

4. Formation of ethics and ideals as attainable goals after disillusionment by the idealized parents.

One may summarize this discussion of the ego ideal by saying that it is strongly narcissistic; it helps set up standards and moral principles, it sets goals for achievement and increase in self-esteem, and finally, it helps set up cathected shifts towards aim-inhibited goals. It does these things by holding out a carrot (shame) instead of a whip (guilt) as does the superego proper.

Summary

1. The term "Ego ideal" was introduced by Freud in 1914.

2. A number of writers, including Freud himself, have at different times emphasized and deemphasized the difference between the Ego ideal and the Superego proper.

3. The Ego ideal represents the sum of the positive indentifications with parental images.

4. Jeanne Lampl-de-groot and other writers feel that the Ego ideal is entirely separate from the Superego.

5. The Ego ideal and the Superego are best considered to be subfunctions of the ego.

6. The Ego ideal is highly narcissistic.

Chapter VI

THE BACKGROUND OF ΣΥΝΕΙΔΗΣΙΣ

Secular background of Συνείδησις

The origin of the concept of συνείδησις must be
sought, not within the sacred writings, but in the corpus of
secular literature as this was the pool out of which the New
Testament idea developed. This was necessitated by the fact
that the word συνείδησις per see is not found in the Old
Testament, although the idea is at times certainly present
(vide 2 Sam. 24:10, Job. 27:6). This absence of the word in
the Old Testament appears to point to a Hellenistic rather
than an Hebraic source of the word.

In this connection a number of scholars have concluded
that συνείδησις is essentially a Stoic term. Pierce,[1]
however, in an exhaustive study of the topic, feels that the
available evidence does not warrant such a conclusion. He points
out that, at the most, there are only three available quotations
from the stoics where the word συνείδησις is used, and of
these the most important was of relatively late origin, being
attributed to Epictetus (born circa A.D. 50), i.e., long after
Paul had already made extensive use of the word within a Christian

_____

[1]C. A. Pierce, Conscience in the New Testament, (London:
SCM Press Ltd., 1955), p. 21.

frame of reference. Similarly, although not actually using
the word συνείδησις   Marcus Aurelius (died A.D. 275) in his
writings did approach the concept of "conscience." This again,
however, cannot be considered evidence for a Stoic background
because of the late date. Pierce stresses the difference
between the Pauline and Stoic concepts. For the Stoics, affect
was something negative, while for Paul, the whole concept of
συνείδησις   was characterized by an emotional element. Pierce
concluded that "it can be summarily stated that while it is
doubtful whether the idea connoted by συνείδησις   is used,
let alone originated by Stoicism, it is quite certain that
συνείδησις   itself is not."[2]

It appears that the term συνείδησις is but one of a
group of cognates or similar words or phrases which were used
interchangeably to express the same idea. The use, for example,
of τῷ ἰδίῳ συνειδότι   in the final sentence of the pseudo-
Epictetus fragment indicates that τό συνειδός   is, there at
least, interchangeable with συνείδησις   This clue, in
addition, leads directly to Stobaeus' chapter, Περί τοῦ
Συνειδοτος   which contains a catena of sixteen apophthegms
called from a wide variety of authors to illustrate the subject.
As relevant to τό συνειδός   this excerptor of the sixth century
A.D. includes quotations which employ:

a) αὐτῷ συνειδέναι τι,

b) αὐτῷ συνιστορεῖν,

---

[2]Ibid., p. 19.

c) σύνεσις,

d) συνείδησις,

e) τό συνειδός

It is from an examination of the use of these words
and phrases during a period of thirteen centuries of Greek
literature that we can discover with reasonable precision the
meaning that συνείδησις   carried when Paul introduced it into
christianity. These words are used over and over again in
Greek literature, from the sixth century B.C. to the seventh
century A.D. They are used by every possible type of author
from philosophers and poets to playwrights and physicians. Thus
in Paul's day, the use of the word συνείδησις was already more
popular than philosophic. Norden,[3] in commenting on the first
appearance of the term in Greek literature, correctly observed
that this was a concept which was not a creation of Democritus.
"It is not a philosophic conception at all, but belongs to the
great and still too little investigated group of ethical concep-
tions which were taken up by ethics as material, but originated
in popular thought."

Another interesting and important aspect of the concept
is that it remained quite static, being relatively little changed
in its long usage. This is also true for the period after the
development of christianity. Stobaeus[4] compiled his catena in
the sixth century A.D. and, with no sense of inconsistency,

---

[3]Ibid., p. 16.

[4]Ibid., p. 17.

included apophthegms from the fourth, fifth and sixth centuries
B.C., as well as from the first century A.D. This indicates
that Paul's concept of συνείδησις was probably very similar
to that within the total matrix out of which the word originally developed.

All the words in this group are probably etymologically
related to σύνοιδα which itself occurs only once in the
New Testament (Acts 5:2). There is, however, a possibility
that Luke in his use of συνιδών (14:16) intended this participle to be understood as standing virtually for an aorist of
σύνοιδα rather than συνοράω although this is by no means
certain. The basic meaning of the word is "I know in common with."
Its more general use, however, is to indicate knowledge about
another person as a potential witness for or against him. From
here there naturally develops the idea of "bearing witness."
Other ideas similarly arise, e.g.:

a) sharing a secret with another;

b) such sharing may lead to complicity and
hence to guilt;

c) the idea of awareness or consciousness of self
or of something else.

An understanding of the phrase and construction αὐτῷ
συνειδέναι is important for an understanding of the use of
the concept in the New Testament. The idea shows signs of the
evolutionary process which has just been considered:

a) to share and know with oneself;

b) to have a personal secret;

c) to be a witness for or against oneself;

d) to bear witness to oneself.

Of the three substantival equivalents for the verbal
phrase:

a) Τό συνειδός   does not occur in the New Testament;

b) σύνεσις   occurs frequently in the New Testament
and Septuagint, but always in the ordinary sense
of "understanding";

c) Συνείδησις   while common enough in non-biblical
Greek, is the most frequently used in the New
Testament.

In his treatise, Pierce[5] demonstrates that:

a) Συνείδησις   is simply an alternative for τό
συνειδος   and for the infrequently used σύνεσις;

b) That these three words are substantival equivalents
for σύνοιδα   but especially for ἐμαυτῷ σύνοιδα.

The question can very legitimately be raised as to why
the New Testament writers evidently preferred συνείδησις   to
the other words or phrases in this group. The probable reason
is that preference for a noun to a verbal phrase is an expected
mark of the popular development of language such as occurred
in the Koine. In addition, συνείδησις   may have been preferred
by the New Testament authors because it was less ambiguous.
There are also some indications that in the "dialect" of the
environment in which the New Testament was written,   συνείδησις

---

[5]Ibid., p. 19.

was already preferentially established even in personal use. Another interesting feature is the observation that the writers who use συνείδησις are predominantly Asiatic in origin while those who prefer τό συνειδος are principally European.

Συνείδησις in the Old Testament and Apocrypha

As has been pointed out, συνείδησις came into the New Testament with its meaning already crystallized. The Greek concept was almost always that of a guilty conscience. Συνείδησις was a judge and was primarily concerned with the affects of guilt and shame.

Occasionally, σύνεσις was used as a synonym for συνείδησις and this usage is quite frequent in the New Testament and Septuagint. It always, however, appears in its ordinary sense of understanding. The other very common synonym for συνείδησις is τό συνειδος but this does not occur at all in the Bible or Apocrypha. Σύνοιδα is rare in the Bible, but does occur in Acts 5:2, 12:12, 14:6. In the Old Testament, it occurs once in Lev. 5:1, where it appears to connote such direct personal knowledge as would consitute the knower a witness--but obtained in some other way than by seeing. In the Apocrypha, it occurs twice, (I. Mac. 4:21; II. Mac. 4:41) and also in III. Mac. 2:8. In none of these cases, however, does it mean much, if anything, other than συνιδόντες and some manuscripts even prefer this reading.

The use of σύνοιδα plus the dative of the reflexive pronoun is germane to this study and occurs twice in the Greek Bible (Job 27:6; I Cor. 4:4). The use in Job is a clear paraphrase of the Hebrew idea. A Greek would have preferred to express the negative by using μή   or one of its compounds with the participle implied or expressed, rather than οὐ with the main verb.

Similarly, συνείδησις   is found in Eccl. 10:20, although the revised version is to be preferred here. There is still no indication, however, of an original Hebrew concept in the text as it stands. The use of the concept in Wisdom 17:11 (R.V.) is also Greek, being used absolutely with reference to wickedness. Here, likewise, an attempt to find a latent Hebrew original is unavailing and, in any case, to deny the Greek background of the passage would be to completely ignore all the available evidence.

Summary

1. ευνείδησις   appears to have an Hellenic, and possibly a Stoic, origin.

2.   There are, however, some important differences between the Stoic use of ευνείδησις and the use of the word in the New Testament.

3. ευνείδησις   is one of a group of cognates which are used to express the same basic idea.

4.   By Paul's time the use of the word ευνείδησις was already popular.

5.   The essential notion of the word is a "knowing oneself together with" something or someone else.

Chapter VII

ΣΥΝΕΙΔΗΣΙΣ   IN THE NEW TESTAMENT

As already noted, the idea of conscience, although
implicit in the Old Testament and Apocrypha, is not there clearly
enunciated. The same is true for the Gospels in the New Testament
and, in fact, the notion of conscience does not become prominent
until the letters of Paul.

Within recent years, following study of the word in
the New Testament, some doubts have been raised regarding the
validity of any doctrine of conscience. Osborne[1] feels that Paul
used the term with the vagueness it possessed in popular Greek
thought, and Pierce[2] condemns the expositions of Rashdall, Kirk,
etc., as being foreign to the New Testament. Conscience, he
claims, can be exalted until it becomes idolatry in the Biblical
sense, i.e., setting up something in the place of God, and it
allows men to be a law unto themselves. An examination of
συνείδησις   is thus clearly essential to a correct perception
of the normative usage of the word in the New Testament.

As has been seen, the word was never a part of the
official Stoic vocabulary. It is not in a Stoic, but in

---

[1]H. Osborne, Conscience in the New Testament Journal
of Theological Studies, Vol. XXXII, pp. 167-179.

[2]C. A. Pierce, Conscience in the New Testament
London: SCM Press Ltd., 1955).

Democritus, precursor of the Epicureans, that one finds the first genuine moral use of the word, in the sense of awareness of one's wickedness. The Stoics, however, did speak of the ἔμφυτος ἔννοια of man, his reason which derived from God or cosmic Reason, and more particularly the δαίμων or ideal self, which gave intuitive knowledge of right and wrong. Roman writers, particularly Seneca, used "conscientia" in a similar sense. Thus to attribute a Stoic origin to the word συνείδησις is strictly a fallacy, but, at the same time, there is no doubt of its connection with Stoic ideas.

There is no need here to go into the question of Paul's contact with hellenistic philosophy. Some scholars have maintained that he only learned what he knew second hand from his Jewish teachers at Jerusalem who used to give summaries of Greek contemporary thought to their pupils, as part of their equipment for the maintenance and defense of the Jewish faith amongst the Diaspora in the Mediterranean world. It is, however, more natural to assume that Paul, even if he was never a student in the philosophical schools of Tarsus, was well aware of their tenets and their vocabulary, as well as of the parlance of the educated classes in his home city and elsewhere.

Συνείδησις was one of the few terms introduced by Paul from the Greek world which had not been already colored by Jewish ideas. It was not well established in popular idiom in the full sense of man's personal awareness of the moral quality of his acts and his character and of the associated idea of guilt. The classical definition in Latin is "ille internus quasi index

qui, quid faciendum fugiendumque sit, edocet (conscientia) atque
bene facta approbat, male facta improbat (conscientia consequens)."

In Romans 2:14-15, is found the "locus classicous" of
Paul's use of the term συνείδησις   Here the moral responsibility of the Jew before God is compared with that of the Gentile.
God judges without respect of persons and according to the knowledge of his truth as it is possessed in measure by all men.
Conscience is here spoken of as distinct from the writing of the
law in the heart since it witnesses to this, giving rise to
thoughts of approval or disapproval in men's minds. S. P. Thorton-
Duesbery expresses the idea well when he describes conscience as
"a second reflective consciousness which a man has alongside his
original consciousness of an act--readily personified."[3]

Mind and conscience are distinct (cf. Titus 1:15) --
νοῦς   is that which creates a purpose or act: συνείδησις   is
that which judges a purpose or act. Pierce[4] analyzes such a use
as "moral, bad, absolute," pointing to the context which is that
of the failure of the Gentiles to live up to the light they have
and the comparable failure of self-righteous Jews. Pierce sees
its nature as essentially negative, the conscience never being
able to say more than "not wrong." Harris[5] insists that this is

---

[3]Article "Conscience" in A Theological Word Book of
the Bible, Editor A. Richardson (London: SCM Press, 1950),
p. 83.

[4]C. A. Pierce, Conscience in the New Testament, London:
SCM Press, 1955.

[5]B. F. Harris, Συνείδησις   in the Pauline Writings
Westminister Theological Journal, No. 24-25, May 1961, pp. 173-186.

going beyond the evidences of this and other passages. The
conscience can, for example, commend as well as condemn. The
reason why its function is so often to condemn is the imperfec-
tion of man, even of the regenerate man; but this alone must
not be considered the normative sense.

Romans 9:1 indicates the validity of this position,
where Paul refers to the additional witness of his conscience
that he is indeed speaking the truth when he declares his great
yearning for his fellow Jews. There is no negative aspect of
conscience required here. Similarly in II Timothy 1:13 Paul
speaks of a "pure conscience." Likewise in the two passages
in Acts where Luke records the addresses of Paul before the
Sanhedrin (23:1) and before Felix (24:16) a negative view is
not required.

The third passage is in Romans 13:15 where Paul is
instructing the Christians in their duties toward the State.
Here conscience is linked immediately with "the wrath," manifested externally through human authority. A negative use does
not seem to exhaust the sense here, in spite of its immediate
connection with ἡ ὀργή   The context allows for a positive
sense also in that one may receive praise from one's conscience.

In Romans, therefore, the conscience is viewed as a
divine gift to all men, which makes explicit in the moral
consciousness of the works of the law of God written in the
heart. Conscience therefore does not possess its own intrinsic
authority: its authority rests in God himself who has given it,
and on his law, the knowledge of which it brings to man's attention

This point is clearly brought out in I Corinthians 4:4 where
Paul is speaking of Christian stewardship: "My own conscience
is clear in the matter--I am not finally accountable to you
Corinthians or to any others. But even the approbation of my
own conscience does not ultimately justify me. He that judgeth
me is the Lord." He is the final authority of the human conscience. I Peter 2:19 confirms this view.

In I Corinthians, Paul had been asked for advice regarding
the problem of eating meats which had been dedicated to idols.
Συνείδησις occurs frequently in Paul's discussion of the
situation. Pierce[6] believes that the appeal to conscience was
something the Corinthians themselves had introduced, and that
Paul somewhat reluctantly answers them in their own language.
Συνείδησις was a claim of his opponents and, says Pierce, he
demonstrates its inadequacy. Certainly Paul is determined not
to allow a spirit of arrogance and superiority and this determination is clearly enunciated in 8:1-3. He does, however,
introduce the idea of συνείδησις naturally enough in verse 7.
Their consciences are still "weak" in the sense that they had
not completely cast off the old associations, and taken their
stand on the principle that "the earth is the Lord's, and the
fullness thereof" (10:26) and that idol-worship has been in fact
the worship of non-existent gods (8:4-6). Paul's clear direction
in this case is that the more mature Christian should not insist
on liberty of conscience and thus offend his weaker brother

---

[6]C. A. Pierce, op. cit, p. 60.

because the latter's conscience would be defiled thereby.

Conscience therefore, gives divergent judgements for Christians on some practical issues in life, according to their differing, i.e., more mature and less mature, apprehension of the will of God. The law of love is therefore appealed to as the overriding dictate of conscience recognized by both weak and strong. In Chapter Ten, a somewhat different problem is raised, namely that of a Christian dining with a non-Christian. Since the meat in question had definitely been dedicated to idols, the Christian must refrain "for conscience sake," i.e., the conscience of the pagan as Paul makes clear in verse 29. What advantage would there be if the liberty exercised by a strong Christian comes under the condemnation of another, either weaker Christian or Pagan? So the same overriding principle is adhered to, the edification and growth in love of all Christians, and the desire for the conversion of the pagans (vv. 32 f.): on these all consciences would agree. For cases of conflict of conscience, Paul would seem to be saying here: let there be an appeal by both parties to some higher more comprehensive dictate of conscience, and let the lesser issue be decided in the light of that.

In 2 Corinthians 1:12, Paul again uses συνείδησις in a context and meaning similar to Roman 9:1. Even Pierce admits that the use of the word here is positive and it is as eloquent an expression as we have anywhere in Paul's writings of the approbation of one's conscience, which follows a godly life and a faithful ministry. The two other examples in II Corinthians,

4:2 and 5:11, are not admitted by Pierce as relevant because
they are non-reflexive in meaning: "'commending ourselves to
everyman's conscience in the sight of God,' the idea of shared
knowledge in συνείδησις here not involving every man with
himself, as it were, but every man and Paul, i.e., the mutual
knowledge, as before God, that Paul has faithfully fulfilled
his ministry."[7]

In the Pastoral Epistles, there are four passages in
I Timothy, four of which, in Pierce's view, are negative. The
first is 1:5, ἀγαθὴ συνείδησις;   love is the τέλος of the
commandment, love which proceeds from a pure heart and a pure
conscience. This context is entirely positive: actual purity
of heart, reflected in an approving conscience, is the essential
condition for the highest fulfillment of the law, the spirit of
love. The same adjective ἀγαθή is used in verse 19: good
conscience here means the inner assurance for Timothy that he
has been waging, and is now waging, the good warfare (v. 18)
which again is the positive sense of the word. Paul, however,
reminds us that this good conscience can be put away in the
course of departing from the faith (vv. 19 f.). Extreme cases
of this are referred to at the beginning of Chapter IV. The
conscience of these reprobates is "seared with a hot iron" -
κεκαυτηριασμένων την ἰδίαν συνείδησιν.

In contrast to this is the remaining passage in the
letter, 3:9, where purity of conscience, καθαρα συνείδησις
is mentioned as a concomitant of faithful adherence to the faith

---

[7]Harris, op. cit., p. 183.

- again a positive sense. The only other reference in the
Pastorals is in Titus 1:15, which describes the opposite state -
μεμίανται αὐτῶν καὶ ὁ νοῦς καὶ ἡ συνείδησις.
There is a solemn ring in these words. Those who have wilfully
turned from the light of God's truth are defiled both in their
minds, at the source of thought and action, and equally in their
consciences, which no longer give them a true assessment of the
rightness and wrongness of their actions in the sight of God.

Moving outside the Pauline corpus, it is noteworthy that
the half-dozen or so passages involving συνείδησις   conform
to Paul's use of the word, and in some instances further elucidate
it.   It occurs five times in the latter chapters of the Epistle
to Hebrews.   There are two references to the καθαρισμος of the
conscience which was unattainable under the sacrificial system
of the Old Order (10:2) but which had now been attained through
the blood of Christ (9:14).   This cleaning of the conscience
follows the exercise of faith and in a sense is progressive; as
the Christian apprehends and obeys more of the truth as it is
in Christ, so the conscience becomes purer.   Verse 22 of Chapter
Ten dwells on the same thought on the negative side - ἐρραντισμένοι
τας καρδίας ἀπο συνειδησεως πονηρᾶς.
The result is a καλὴ συνείδησις   as it occurs in the final
reference in 13:18, the honorable conscience which is the concomitant of honorable living.

The Authorized Version does contain a single reference
in the Gospels to conscience, in the Adulteress Pericope at the
beginning of John Chapter VIII.   This incident, while usually

taken to be authentic, is not regarded by many scholars as part
of the original Gospel, and the phrase "being corrected by their
own conscience:" has even less claim to be included, since it
is in all probability a gloss following five uncial MSS of the
sixth century and later. Pierce[8] takes the whole incident,
however, as illustrative of his general view of συνείδησις
The woman, because she had transgressed the moral law, was in
danger of the wrath mediated by human institutions, the penalty
of death. Her accusers, however, were shown by the Lord to be
themselves subject through their sinful hearts to the wrath
mediated internally through the pangs of conscience.

In the New Testament, then, the term συνείδησις is used
naturally and without definition. There is some lack of precision
in meaning here and there, because the word was already well
established in natural parlance at the time, and had the same
lack of precision often seen in words in ordinary use.

Osborne concludes as follows: "I find no justification
for the view of certain scholars that the word and concept sustained at his (Paul's) hands an enrichment and development of
meaning, apart of course, from the new and higher ethical valua-
tions which were attendant upon the Christian renewal, and which
incidently affect the judgement of what constitutes a good or
bad conscience."[9] This would not seem to be an entirely accurate

---

[8]Pierce, op. cit., p. 105.

[9]H. Osborne, Conscience in the New Testament, Journal
of Theological Studies, Vol. XXXII, pp. 167-170.

perception of the situation. Surely Paul did enrich and develop
the sense of the word, particularly on the positive side, i.e.,
the place of conscience in the experience of the Christian.
It is on this side that this author believes Pierce's analysis
is defective in spite of the thoroughness of his investigation.
No one would maintain that conscience is an important doctrine,
so that it is unnecessary for Osborne to point out that Paul
attempted no integration of συνείδησις with the doctrine of
repentance, and faith and love. The conscience is part of the
equipment, as it were, given to men by God for the realization
of his truth in personal experience. It is therefore holy,
and is designed to be as the voice of God within, but is to be
distinguished from the truths it mediates.

It is true that the most frequent use of συνείδησις
in the New Testament involves the consciousness of sin, and
warning against infringement of God's laws, and that it usually
refers to the past and present, i.e., that "conscientia consequens
moralis" is often the case. There is, however, the other side,
and conscience in the non-Christian can still provide considerable knowledge of God's standards for the life; much more in
the Christian, if it is pure and enlightened and sensitive to
his voice. In the Christian it can give an inner assurance and
peace when that voice is obeyed. Conscience, therefore, does
play its part in any account of the Christian life as God intends
it to be lived.

Summary

1.   In the New Testament the concept of conscience does not become prominent until the writings of Paul.

2.   Within recent years some writers have claimed that Paul used the term συνείδησις with the vagueness it possessed in secular Greek thought and that no clear doctrine of συνείδησις in the New Testament is possible.

3.   Συνείδησις is not a Stoic term and it is rather in Democritus that the first clearly moral use of the word is found.

4.   It is clear that Paul must have had first hand knowledge with Hellenestic philosophic concepts.

5.   The term συνείδησις , as used by Paul to indicate moral awareness, was not already colored by Jewish ideas.

6. Συνείδησις   is distinct from the cardiac law in Romans 2:14-15.

7.   The concept of conscience is used by Paul with both positive and connotations.

8.   Conscience may give divergent judgements according to its degree of maturity.

9.   The use of συνείδησις outside the Pauline Corpus tends to conform to Paul's usage.

10.   The term συνείδησις appears to have been used just as it was being used in everyday language.

Chapter VIII

A PSYCHOLOGICAL EXAMINATION OF ΣΥΝΕΙΔΗΣΙΣ
IN THE NEW TESTAMENT

Any accurate knowledge which may be attained regarding
life and man's composite being will ultimately be in harmony
with Biblical revelation. The same God is the author of both.
The written revelation was given to inform man how, when, where
and why he was created, and also to instruct him concerning the
nature, character and personality of his Creator. This revelation, not only unfolds God to man, but it also in a large
measure, explains man to himself. It discriminates and differentiates between his manifold powers and divinely divides and
declares his spiritual, mental and physical proportions.[1]

Psychoanalytic theory teaches that conscience develops
as a result of the moral code which society formulated for its
own protection. Violations of the code were so severely punished
by the tribe that men were afraid to perform any anti-social act.
There is much truth to this position, for so often conscience
does in fact operate to prevent a course of action which would
be followed by pain or displeasure. It is not always so, however,
for sometimes conscience demands, despite the ensuing pain, the
confession of some thing which was unlikely ever to be discovered.

---

[1]Thomas Baird, Conscience (New York: Charles C. Cook,
1914), p. 19.

Many have even gone to martyrdom rather than violate their conscience.

The Bible says that there is in man an innate moral sense which acts as an "indicator," registering the rightness or wrongness of a thought or action. The key reference in Scripture is Romans 2:15 where Paul says that the Gentiles "shew the work of the law written in their hearts, their conscience bearing witness therewith, and their thoughts one with another accusing or else excusing them." (Vide Fig. I) The conscience and "cardiac law" may be regarded as a vestigial and additional parameter of consciousness, an "apparatus for feeling" of the personality. (Vide Fig. I) They, together, point out those things within an individual which are conducive to the well-being of the personality and warns against others. In other words, they are the sensory part of the spiritual "protective reflex." They may be enlightened and taught by the Word of God. Also, while the "cardiac law," in contrast to the conscience proper, cannot be regarded as simply a faculty acquired from our environment, it is certainly capable of reinforcement by the correct use of experience. The interplay of choices associated with internal disciplines of psychological processes is particularly powerful in this respect. External disciplines, whether in the form of social sanctions or church disciplines also play their part.[2]

In the Bible, the almost absolute silence of the Old

---

[2]O. Hallesby, Conscience (London: Inter-Varsity Fellowship, 1955).

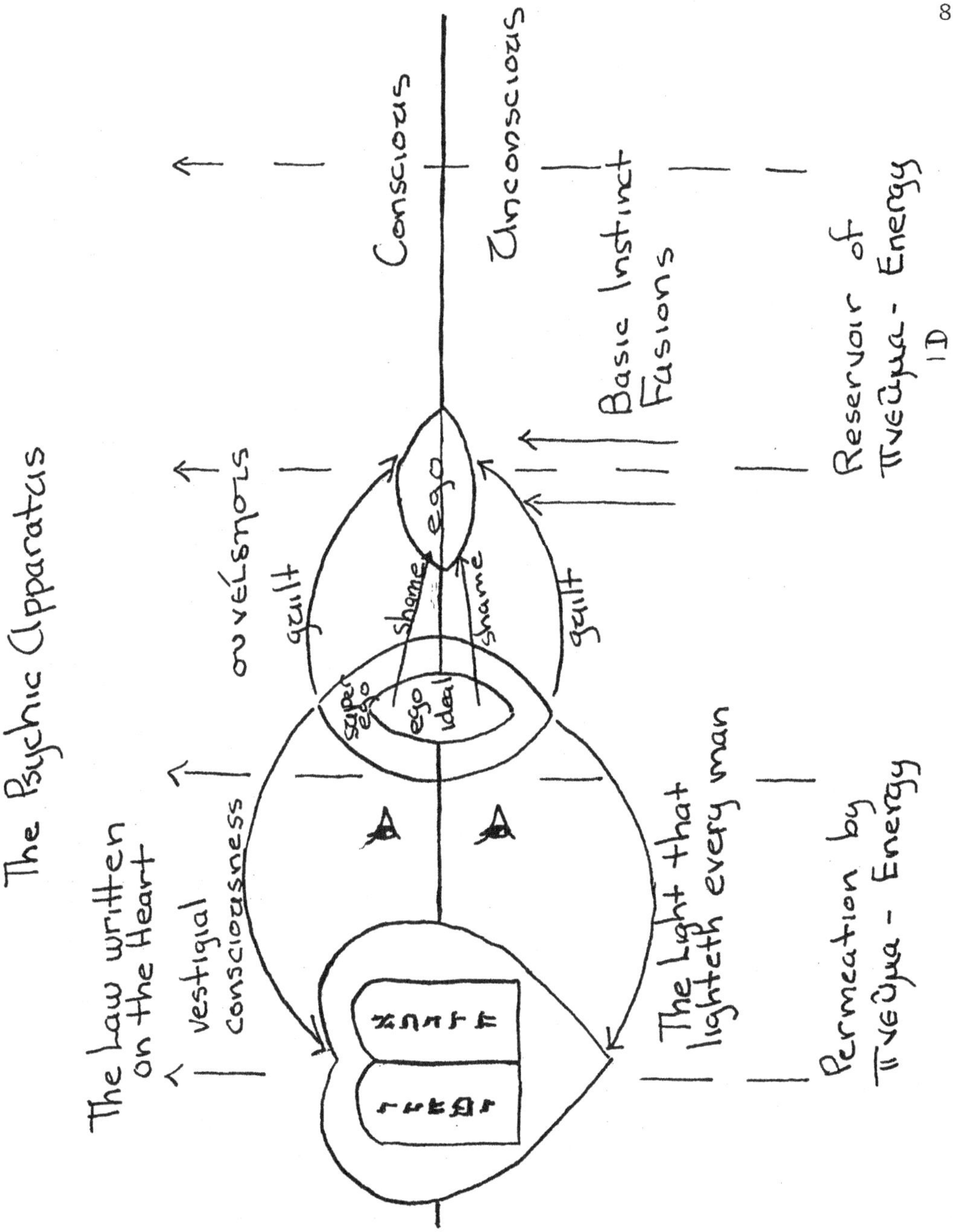

The Psychic Apparatus

Conscious

Unconscious

Basic Instinct Fusions

Reservoir of πνεῦμα - Energy
ID

overtones

guilt

shame

ego

super ego

ego ideal

shame

guilt

The Law written on the Heart

vestigial consciousness

The light that lighteth every man

Permeation by πνεῦμα - Energy

88

Fig. I

Testament on the subject of conscience must remain an impene-
trable mystery. Only once in the range of the Old Testament
revelation is conscience directly referred to, and then it is
relegated to a marginal position. (Eccl. 10:29). The thought,
however, is there, and is usually expressed by the word "heart."
Thus, for example, I Samuel 24:5: "And it came to pass afterward
that David's heart smote him, because he had cut off Saul's
skirt."

In the New Testament, the word conscience is used very
frequently, especially by Paul and the author of Hebrews. The
Old Testament expression "heart" is also used in several
instances. Thus I John 3:19-20 reads: "And hereby we know
that we are of the truth, and shall assure our heart before him.
For if our heart condemns us, (i.e. if guilt or shame is produced)
God is greater than our heart and knoweth all things." Here there
can be no doubt that heart means conscience and the same is true
for Mark 3:5.

Conscience, as has been demonstrated, is not merely a
knowing, a consciousness, but a knowing together with something
or someone and in particular with the innate "cardiac law."
Among all races it is characteristic of man that he in his "cardiac
law" knows together with a will that is over and above his own,
a supernatural, supramundane, superpowerful will, which makes
demands upon his will, and which has a right to do so. This will,
which is the will of God, the "cardiac law," is what men call the
law. It is the moral law according to which man's life should
be lived. Conscience can, therefore, be defined as that knowledge

or consciousness by which man knows that he is conforming to the moral law, to the will of God, or to the innate "cardiac law."

Conscience expresses itself sometimes before, sometimes during, and sometimes after the act involved. Before, it either encourages one to carry out a contemplated action, or advises one not to do it. During the act, the voice of conscience is generally weakest. That is when it is most difficult for conscience to make itself heard because attention and psychic energy are directed else-where. After the act conscience usually speaks most strongly, either approving the deed and expressing satisfaction with it, or protesting against it and producing inner unrest and anxiety. In the former instance, one speaks of "a good conscience" in the latter of "a bad conscience." Both of these expressions are, however, misleading, inasmuch as it is not the conscience which is good or bad, but the judgement and in particular, the affect which is produced. One's conscience is equally good whether it expresses approval or disapproval of an act, just as a barometer may be equally good, whether it indicates "stormy" or "fair." A "good" conscience therefore, refers to the "good" effect which its judgement registers upon the individual, the feeling of pleasure or pain which it produces.

In order to integrate adequately the insights of modern psychology with the revelation of inspired scripture, it may be helpful to consider the psychic apparatus in a schematic manner. The pre-requisite to such an integration is the recognition that the term συνείδησις is inclusive of both the Superego proper and the Ego ideal. When this distinction is kept clearly in mend a psychotheological approach to the exegesis of those passages containing the word συνείδησις may then be attempted with some degree of confidence, as long as we do not fall into the trap of believing that the model is reality. The model is merely a conceptualization to help one describe and perhaps understand the phenomenal world.

An examination of the diagram in Fig. I. may make this somewhat clearer. This particular model represents the basic psychic apparatus as viewed within the psychoanalytic frame of reference. There is a level of consciousness and a level of the unconscious and the Ego, as the executive agent of the personality, mediates between these two levels and between them and external reality. The Id is the reservoir of the basic energy of the human personality and is closely related to the πνεῦμα which makes the body a living personality or soul. The Superego and the Ego ideal together form the New Testament συνείδησις and have both conscious and unconscious components. The Superego proper controls the executive activities of the Ego by the production of or absence of guilt-anxiety. Similarly, the Ego ideal controls the activities of the Ego, not by a whip as does the Superego, but by the carrot of shame-anxiety or its absence, namely, approbation.

In the opinion of this author, the συνείδησις is learned in charter and its content. One of its functions, however, is, by means of a vestigial consciousness, to be "knowing with" the divinely given and innate law written on the heart which Paul carefully distinguishes from the συνείδησις proper. It would appear that this "cardiac law" and the vestigial consciousness of it may well represent the post-fall "light that lighteth every man that cometh into the world" (John 1:9).

The sequence of action for any activity is then as follows:

1.   An instinctual pressure for discharge and fulfillment exists in the unconscious.

2.   As this nears consciousness it produces anxiety, which is perceived by the Ego. This, in turn, forces the Ego to face the decision whether to permit the expression of the instinct or to repress it or to handle it in some other defensive way.

3.   The learned Superego proper may signal to the Ego that the expression of such an instinct is taboo or inappropriate by the production of guilt-anxiety. This will cause the Ego to call into play a defense mechanism, which mostly likely, will be repression.

4.   The Ego ideal, on the other hand, may signal to the Ego that the expression of such instinctual activity would not be in agreement with the values and standards of the introjected idealized images which have gone into its formulation.

5.   While this is going on the complete συνείδησις , if healthy and unhindered, is casting the eye of vestigial consciousness to the divinely implanted "law written in the heart" or mind to discover if such instinctual expression should be approved or condemned by the innate moral barometer.

Frequently, an examination of the use of συνείδησις
in the New Testament from a psychoanalytic point of view sheds
additional light on the exact concept the author was attempting
to communicate. An attempt will be made to do this in a few
instances and to correlate the psychological and the theological use of the concept of conscience.

Romans 2:14, 15 (R.S.V.)

"When the Gentiles who have not the law do by nature
what the law requires, they are a law unto themselves, even
though they do not have the law. They show that what the law
requires is written on their hearts, while their conscience
also bears witness and their conflicting thoughts accuse or
perhaps excuse them."

Here Paul gives a description of what might in theological language be called conscience in the natural man. This
faculty antedates the process of introjection or even of the
inhibition of sadism which, as has been demonstrated, is the
precursor of the Freudian superego. According to Paul, the
"cardiac law" described would appear to be the birthright
possession of every human being and is, therefore, inherent in
all mankind. The conscience proper, however, is not this set
of moral statutes written in the heart or mind of every human
being. Rather the conscience is the spiritual consciousness
of such a moral code and frequently witnesses to it by calling
attention to it. This consciousness may well be a vestigial
remnant of the Imago Dei and, as previously indicated, appears
to function as "the light that lighteth every man that cometh

into the world." The quantity and quality of the introjects which go into the making of the conscience proper may later modify this vestigial remnant by heightening or lowering the level of its functioning and thus the individual's perception of the "cardiac law." If the conscience proper is alive and sensitive, or more accurately, if one is sensitive to it, and it has not been strangulated and atrophied by numerous weak and vacillating introjects, it will immediately convict man of wrong thoughts or deeds, that is, wrong as measured against the innately planted moral standard of the law written on the heart.

Often it is not so much a question of knowing right from wrong, but of possessing the strength to respond appropriately. After the Fall, our first-parents certainly did know good and evil but they knew the good while having diminished power to do it. Similarly they knew the evil without having the available strength to resist the evil. This lack of strength in the natural man, however, is not a defect in conscience per se, but in psychoanalytic language, constitutes a defect in ego strength. In the Christian, there is the potential to overcome this defect through utilization of the strengthening and modifying effects of the permeating and sealing Spirit (Ephesians 1:13). The natural conscience is therefore pregenital and previous to any differentiation within the psychic matrix. It is an innate reflecting consciousness of "good and evil."

A Defiled Conscience, Titus 1:15 (R.S.V.)

"To a pure all things are pure, but to the corrupt
and unbelieving nothing is pure; their very minds and consciences are corrupted."

The old verb μιαίνω is used only here, in Jude 8
and in Hebrews 12:15. It means to dye with another color or
to stain. As the administration of certain chemicals can
depress the level of the consciousness mediated by the cerebral
cortex and reticular activating system, so continued partici-
pation in the "wrong" or impure" can depress or "stain" the
level of consciousness of the remnant of vestigial consciousness
as well as the introjects in the συνείδησις . The conscience
remains but the reflex rejecting function, with which it operates,
has been grossly impaired.

Something of the same order can be seen in the case
of the superego. At first, the internalized representation of
the parental images with their "do's" and "don'ts" may be highly
cathected and obeyed. If under some influence, such as for
example alcohol, the ego strengths are somewhat dissolved and
an action against the superego code is permitted, then the
repetition of a similar action will become easier for the ego on
a later occasion.

An Evil Conscience, Hebrews 10:22 (R.S.V.)

"Let us draw near with a pure heart in full assurance
of faith, with our hearts sprinkled clean from an evil conscience...."

Here a state of purity of mind is linked to the process
of regeneration as mediated by faith. Such a process by insti-

tuting a state of freedom from forensic guilt allows the individual existentially and experientially to achieve freedom
from affective guilt as well. The conscience per se is never
evil or good but the affects it can liberate through its associated reflections may be pleasurable or unpleasurable. The
cleansing blood of Christ can regenerate the mind to the point
that the clouding effects of narcissism and pleasure principle
pressures can be controlled. It is not the conscience which
is evil, but the filtering influences of sin and instinctual
derivatives which render it relatively inoperative.

A purged conscience, Hebrews 9:14 (R.S.V.)

"How much more shall the blood of Christ, who through
the eternal Spirit offered himself without blemish to God,
purify your conscience from dead works to serve the living God."

In this section, the activity of the Spirit appears
to be connected with the lack of blemish or defect in Christ
and to the possibility of purification of the human conscience.
This conscience was not evil in the sense that a filter of negative material had come between the superego and ego and thus
had effectively reduced the effective power of the conscience.
Here, rather, the conscience or Superego of the individual had
become impaired in that the Ego ideal remained excessively
narcissistic. Such individuals were preoccupied with their own
narcissistic endeavors and thus the quality of their ideal
aspirations was in question. This had also caused a weakening
of the reflecting power of the conscience, not by building a

filter around it, but by narcissistically influencing one of its components.

The Pacified Conscience, Hebrews 10:2 (R.S.V.)

"If the worshipers had been cleansed, they would no longer have any consciousness (συνείδησις) of sin."

In this verse, the author visualizes a state of psychic harmony and integration resulting from the regenerating influence of the Spirit. After a process of cleansing occurs, the filters surrounding the natural conscience, acquired by experiential and inter-personal contacts, are, in some measure, dissolved so that the reflecting power of conscience is less impaired. Forensic guilt has been removed and the superego can never again torment this ego with the thought of past unforgiven transgression against the moral code. For the future the Spirit has strengthened the ego and in cases of failure, no prolonged guilt has to be suffered because the cleansing aspect of Christ's sacrifice remains available.

A good conscience, I Peter 3:16 (R.S.V.)

"Keep your conscience clear, so that, when you are abused, those who revile your good behavior in Christ, may be put to shame."

Six times over in the New Testament is such a clear uninterrupted and unimpaired, rejecting spiritual consciousness described. The High Priest commanded those who stood near to smite Paul on the mouth for asserting that he possessed a good conscience. It is noteworthy that Paul possessed a good conscience before his conversion (Acts 23:1). He also affirms that he actually attained a pure conscience while he was a Pharisee (2 Timothy 1:3). This statement seems quite incompatible with the bitter persecuting spirit which he manifested toward the disciples of Jesus, but it appears that even then, Paul ego-wise was not acting against the moral code as he saw it. A difficulty remains, however, in that his "good" conscience approved actions which were only "good" to a somewhat perverted perception of the moral code. The solution to the difficulty is that at that time, Paul is describing his conscience within a Pharisaic frame of reference. His conscience was good insofar as he obeyed the introjects which formed it.

For the Christian, the possibility of a clear unimpaired reflecting functioning of the conscience remains a possibility. When one has attained this state, it appears that one can become a more effective witness causing others to see the inadequacy of their Ego ideals and thus causing them to experience shame.

The convicting conscience, John 8:9 (A.V.)

"And when they heard it, being convicted by their own conscience, went out one by one, beginning with the eldest, even unto the last..."

Even though the authenticity of this section is in question, it is useful as an example of the action of conscience. The conscience rendered ineffective by a filter of sin, is like creation in chaos, that is, its illuminating reflecting action towards the Ego is negated. As the Spirit begins to operate, the ego-reflecting power of conscience is increased and the ego begins to experience affective guilt. The individual is convicted affectively. At that point, if he sees the inadequacies in his idealized self-image, he will also experience shame. The central thesis of the Christian position is that when this position is reached affectively and forensically, the Spirit can then mediate relief.

Other examples of the use of συνείδησις may likewise be viewed within an analytic frame of reference and additional exegetical insight gained. Thus it is possible to wound the consciences of others (I Corinthians 8:12) by our actions. As models of identifications for others, one may become inadequate and thus disrupt their Ego ideals and Superegos. The reflected voice of conscience may become weak (I Corinthians 8:12) and completely filtered out and this intra-psychic filter may become so thick and effective that the conscience can best be described as seared (I Timothy 4:2) and inoperative and in the final stages of such practice, as completely abandoned (I Timothy 1:19). It is possible for an individual to reach a point where he behaves as if he was without conscience or "cardiac law."

It may be useful to note that much of the disagreement between such writers as Pierce and Harris regarding whether the conscience is essentially negative or whether it can be positive appears to be based on a failure to differentiate between the Superego proper and the Ego ideal and thus between shame and guilt. Thus in Romans 9:1 it is Paul's Ego ideal which is reflecting on the fact that Paul is living up to the standard of the introjected Christ in refusing to lie. Similarly in 2 Timothy 1:3 it is Paul's Ego ideal which stands as a witness that Paul has served God with all the persistence and faithfulness which characterized the introjected images of his parents and forefathers. Paul's Ego ideal has also been met by all of Paul's actions as he stands before the Sanhedrin (Acts 23:1) and Felix (24:16) so Paul's συνείδησις remains "good" and "void of offense."

In Romans 13:5 both the Ego ideal and Superego proper aspects of συνείδησις are in view. The Ego ideal is active when we "do that which is good" and we then experience the good feeling of having lived up to the ideals of the introjected images. In such a situation the good feeling is marked by the absence of shame and by the fact that "thou shalt have praise of the same."

In I Cor. 8:7 the apostle speaks of the conscience being "weak" and "defiled." This is a good example of the difference between the two parts of συνείδησις . The Ego ideals of the young Corinthian Christians were still in a very immature and formative stage and the values and standards of their introjects still, as yet, had not been fully assimilated. The Ego ideal conscience was therefore still weak. The Superego conscience was, however, not weak but defiled.

They had engaged in activities which resulted not only in shame (weakness) but in defilement (guilt). Paul's point is that mature Christians will say "no" to certain perfectly legal ego-choices because of the high standards of their Ego

ideal introjects which say - "Do not engage in that which,
though for you it is free of guilt or shame, may well result
in shame reactions in those who are less mature."

In 2 Cor. 1:12, Paul very clearly refers to the testimony
of his Ego ideal conscience. The reaction of the conscience
in this instance is to flood the Psyche with the good feeling
of approbation and freedom from shame-anxiety because Paul has
not failed to live in the word as the Christ introject would
direct.

As has been demonstrated, the Ego ideal is an important
element in the conscience and Superego. It appears that as a
result of the regenerating activity of the Spirit, the whole
psychic apparatus is permeated. This will result in increased
ego strength to deal with instinctual pressures in the light of
the reflections of conscience. In addition, it appears there
is a radical modification of the narcissistically oriented Ego
ideal. Instead of the Ego ideal remaining on the level of its
precursor, the primary narcissism, it gains a new dimension,
namely, the introjected image of Christ, his values and aspirations. This then is the image the Christian will aspire towards
and Paul's reminder of "Christ in you" thus becomes a meaningful
reality. Similarly, if one fails in such an aspiration one in
the present stands before Him ashamed even as one shall more
concretely stand with shame, as an eschatological reality.

Summary

1. Since all truth is one, the validated findings of
science will always be in agreement with the inspired revelation

of the Holy Spirit who is truth.

2. The συνείδησις and the "cardiac law," although distinct, act in harmony with in the personality.

3. The word for conscience is, surprisingly, almost completely absent from the Old Testament, but, however, it is found frequently in the New Testament.

4. Conscience is a "knowing with" a law authority, namely, "the cardiac law."

5. Συνείδησις may be either "good" or "bad."

6. The "cardiac law" would appear to be the birthright of every person.

7. The συνείδησις may be defiled or evil in terms of the behavioral it tends to stimulate.

8. Similarly the συνείδησις may be purged, pacified, good, and convicting.

9. Confusion results in exegesis when the Superego and the Ego ideal are not differentiated.

Chapter IX

THE GREEK CONCEPT OF SOUL

The origin of an idea or concept often gives some clue
as to its value and while history cannot prove the orthodoxy
or truth of a doctrine, it may supply much valuable information
and insight. The first clear occurrence of the concept of the
soul as something separate from, and yet closely related to
the physical body, was, according to Herodotus, among the Egyptians. It is true that the early Egyptian teaching on the nature
and immortality of the soul was not exactly the same as what is
usually considered to be the orthodox position in modern theological thinking, but this teaching appears to be clearly related
to later Greek ideas which have in turn strongly influenced
modern theological thought. Much of Egyptian teaching in this
regard amounted to only a soul-survival for a limited period,
namely, so long as the body or the form of the body could be
preserved. This accounts for the sandgraves, the mummies and
the pyramids of Egypt. This particular belief was also often
linked with metempsychosis, namely, the concept of the transmigration of souls.

The ψυχή   in Homer (8th Century B.C.)

In early Greek literature there is no word for the
later notions of body and soul. σῶμα was simply the corpse and

103

the living organisms was denoted by a variety of plural expressions. In all probability the earliest instance of σῶμα being used for "The living human body" is in Hesiod.[1]

The word ψυχή appears in Greek literature as early as 900 B.C. and was etymologically related to ψύχω which means to blow or cool and to ψῦχος cold. Like these words have obvious qualities of onomatopoiea. The word was used to indicate the vital force which resides in the body and which is expressed in the breath. This animating life force produced consciousness, which manifested itself in respiration and the loss of which was synonymous with death. Thus Homer stated that the ψυχή leaves men at the moment of death by escaping through the mouth and in battle the life or ψυχή may be in danger.[2] An early example of this usage is found in Xenophon: "and now because you submitted you saved your lives (ψυχή)"[3]

The ψυχή , in addition, after death goes to the under-world[4] and may sometimes show itself to a living person in a dream prior to burial of the corpse at which time it may take on the appearance of a living man.[5]

It should also be noted that in Homer the ψυχή was specifically human. In the case of an animal it was συμός not ψυχή , which departed at death. As the concept of ψυχή

---

[1]Kittel, Theological Dictionary of the New Testament, No. IX, p. 609.

[2]Homer, Iliad, Vol. 9, p. 408.

[3]Xenophon, Cyropaedia, Vol. 4, No. 4, P. 10.

[4]Homer, Iliad, Vol. 5, p. 654.

[5]Homer, Iliad, Vol. 23, p. 106.

continued to expand it gradually did take on connotations rather similar to modern, though non-biblical concepts, and gradually was associated with the idea of retribution in the hereafter. This notion became widespread from the 7th century B.C. onwards and from about 500 B.C. onward the word ψυχή came to be commonly used as an ominibus term for the total psychological functioning of man as well as for the essential core of man which can be separated from his body and which does not share in the dissolution of the body. As in the oldest available stratum of Orphic and Pythagorean speculation, there develops the dichotomous idea of σῶμα/σῆμα with the body being the tower of the soul.

The ψυχή in Pythagoras (B.C. 580-505)

Pythagoras is said to have spent thirty years in foreign countries, studying with the priests of Egypt, the Magi of Persia, and the gymnosophists of India. He taught the pre-existence and transmigration of souls; that no real entity was made or destroyed; and that, as a consequence, the souls of men are eternal. He was the great pioneer of Greek philosophy.

ψυχή in Plato (B.C. 429-347)

The works of Plato may be categorized according to the time they were written.

Early Period

1. Phaedo

2. Gorgias

3. Symposium

Middle Period

1. The Republic

2. Phaedrus

3. Theaetetus

Late Period

1. Timaeus

2. Philebus

3. Laws

It will be useful, therefore, to examine a representative work from each period of Plato's life in order to gain a view of his concept of soul.

Charles has strongly contended that the concept of innate immortality of the soul, and this automatically involves a view of the soul as a disparate entity, was not a part of Plato's thinking in his early years. He states that "the immortality of the soul was not originally a part of Plato's system. We have in the Republic the various stages through which his views passed before he arrived at his manifest convictions."[6]

A study of Plato's works will show a definite change in Plato's view of the soul. In the Timaeus he is concerned with the soul's divine origin; in the Phaedrus the prior existence of the soul is discussed as is the soul as a principle of motion; and in the Phaedo we find the first evidence of the complete development of the soul as an entity that has a separate existence after death. The same concept is seen, in addition, although in

---

[6]Charles, R. H., A Critical History of the Doctrine of the Future Life, p. 152.

a less well developed form in some of Plato's other works. For example, there is a definite indication of a trichotomous view of man in Alcibiades i (130). There is a discussion as to whether man is one of three things and whether the soul, body or both form the whole.[7]

In Plato's Phaedo there is an account of a discussion which Socrates is supposed to have held when he was in his condemned cell. It is during the course of this discussion that the classical Greek view of the soul is expounded, a view which is not far removed from the traditional idea of the soul in modern Christian thinking.[8] Cullman has summarized this traditional viewpoint quite accurately when he says the "body is only an outer garment which, as long as we live, prevents our soul from moving freely and from living in conformity to it's chains, since it leads the soul out of the prison of the body."[9] This particular conception of the soul as a separate non-physical entity, distinct from the body, was more fully developed at a later date by the Neoplatonists, especially Plotinus and Proclus and it was this view which was later to greatly influence Christian thinking on this subject.[10]

---

[7]Benjamin Jowett, (Translator). The Dialogues of Plato, p. 766.

[8]J. K. Howard, The Concept of the Soul in Psychology and Religion, Journal of the American Scientific Affiliation, Vol. 24, No. 4, December, 1972.

[9]O. Cullman, Immortality of the Soul or Resurrection of the Dead, London, 1958, p. 19.

[10]C. Bigg, The Christian Platonists of Alexandra, Oxford, 1968.

Froom also gives a touching account of that final scene.
The immortality of the soul is here set forth with touching
background and pathetic setting. It presents Socrates and his
friends in prison, the cheerfulness of the victim, the distress
of his friends, the emotion of the jailer. Socrates, the philosopher does not fear death--which he repeatedly declares to be
the "separation of soul from body" in which it is encased--because
he had repressed the lusts that had beset his embodied soul. He
felt himself prepared in his pagan way. And now he welcomes
death as "the final step in an initiation into true being." And
this position was acknowledged to be in sharp contrast with the
current belief of the masses that "the human soul is no more than
the physical breath which death disperses."[11]

It is worthy of note that this was a new notion which
Socrates was expressing, at least in as far as the majority of
the population was concerned. This popular Greek scepticism
was ably expressed by Cebes, a companion of Socrates.

> But men are very incredulous of what you have said of
> the soul. They fear that she will no longer exist anywhere
> when she has left the body, but that she will be destroyed
> and perish on the very day of death. They think that the
> moment that she is released and leaves the body, she will
> be dissolved and vanish away like breath or smoke, and
> thenceforth cease to exist at all.[12]

For the Greek common man the ψυχή was still synonymous with an
individual's life or breath.

In the late works of Plato, we have the development of

11L. Edwin Froom, The Conditionalist Faith of our Fathers,
Vol. I, p. 575.

12Benjamin Jowett, (Translator). The Dialogues of Plato,
p. 15.

his fanciful ideas as to the nature of the soul. In the Laws and in Phaedrus the soul is described as a mystical composite, possessing higher and lower elements. This is in marked contrast to the Phaedo where the soul is seen as one and indivisible. In addition, the soul is now described as being tripartite in nature, like a pair of horses under the control of the charioteer, "Intellect." In addition, in his second speech, Socrates propounds the view that every soul is immortal since it possesses inherent motion.

Shortly before his death at age seventy (Circa. 347 B.C.) Plato discusses the nature of the universe and also of man. Plato's deals in depth with his notions of cosmology and how the universe was formed. He began with the creation of the world by the mythical Demiurge. The creator himself, however, prepared the disparate immortal souls of men which were considered to be unchangeable and imperishable.[13]

The concepts of ψυχή in Plato may be summarized as follows:

1. Socrates continues to use ψυχή in the manner in which the concept had been proceding developmentally as a separate non-physical entity.

2. The soul had three constituent parts:
   a) λογιστικόν
   b) θυμοειςές
   c) επιθυμητικόν

3. λογιστικόν is related to thought, while

[13]Benjamin Jowett, Plato's Timaeus, The Library of Liberal Arts, No. 14, pp. 52-53.

επισυμη-πκόν   is bound to the sense world which does not enjoy true being.

4.   Since the soul, or its pre-eminent part, belongs to transcendent being it is not bound by the finitude of the sense world and is both pre-existent and immortal. At this point it should also prove valuable to present in summary form some of the foundational notions of the psychology of post-platonic philosophy:

A.   Constitution of the Soul

1.   With a few exceptions the Platonists considered the immortality of the soul as a part of intelligible being.

2.   The Peripatetics viewed the immaterial soul as the principle of the form, life and activity of the total organism since there is no separate intelligible being in Aristotelian ontology.

3.   The Epicureans and Stoics considered the soul to be material like all being, whether made up of mobile atoms or like the energy-equivalent πνεῦμα .

4.   The individual soul is simply a broken off part of the world soul with which it will be reunited at death.

B.   Division of the Soul

The Platonic Trichotomy is the starting point of all later divisions. The rational sphere of the soul is specifically human; man shares the irrational and impulsive aspects with animals, and the vegetative sphere he shares with plants and animals.

C.   Popular Ideas of the Post-Classical Age

1. The notion of ψυχή had by this stage developed many of the concepts that were later to be absorbed, from secular heathen Greek thought, into Christian thinking.

2. The ψυχή is the impalpable essential core of man, the bearer of thought, will and emotion, the quintessence of human life.

ψυχή in Philo (Circa 20 B.C. - 54 A.D.)

Philo used the word ψυχή with the meaning of earthly life:

> It is worth inquiring what courage is mentioned in the second place, self-mastery in the third, and prudence in the first, and why he had not set forth a different order of virtues. We must observe then that our soul ψυχή is threefold (τριμερής ἡ ψυχή) and has the rational, the emotional and appetitive desires. And we discover that the head is the place and abode of the rational part, the breast of the emotional part, and the abdomen the seat of the appetite or lustful part; and to each of the part a virtue proper to it has been attached; prodence to the rational part, for it belongs to reason to have knowledge of the things we ought to do and of the things we ought not; courage to the emotional part; self-mastery that we heal and cure our desires.

> As then the head is the first and the highest part of the living creature, the breast the second, and the abdomen the third, and again of the soul the reasoning faculty is first, the high spirited or emotional second, the lustful third; so, too, of the virtues: first is prudence which has its sphere in the first part of the soul which is the domain of reason, and in the first part of the body, namely the head; and second is courage, for it has its seat in the emotions, the second part of the soul and in the breast the corresponding part of the body; and third, self-mastery for its sphere of action is the abdomen, which is, of course, the third part of the body, and the lustful faculty, to which has been assigned the third place in the soul.[14]

Here we have a soul which corresponds in form to the various parts of the physical body.

---

[14]Philo, The Law of Allegory, I.S. 22.

Philo also uses ψυχή in a broader sense to mean the
real and total person:

> In which account, thinking that everything which he
> invited to himself and embraced as a living soul ψυχή
> having considered it equal to the soul, this became the
> name not only of the thing that was thus invited, but
> also of him who invited it in.[15]

Philo also speaks of the death of the man and the death of the
soul as two kinds: "Now the death of man is a separation of
his soul from his body, but the death of the soul is destruction
of virtue and the admission of vice." Philo thus takes the
position that the soul differs from the body and thus espouses
a view which is very close to the traditional view of the soul
as an entity distinct and separate from the body.

Philo as a well trained philosopher had read widely
and was familiar with the Platonic division of the soul into
three parts and with Aristotle's division into eight parts.
He identified the upper and rational part of the soul with the
νοῦς while the lover and irrational part he considered to be
related to the blood. Philo also believed that the οὐσία
of the soul or its νοῦς or λογισμός was the divine πνεῦμα.
In accordance with current philosophical notions Philo felt that
it was only through the highest part of the soul that man could
achieve union with God.

Plutarch (46-120 A.D.)

In Plutarch's lives the ψυχή is translated as both
spirit and soul. He uses the word in the sense of the seat of

---

[15]Philo, The Law of Allegory, II 2.6.

affect: "Thus we see that neither grief nor fear transports and agitates the soul (ψυχή) as much as joy that comes unexpectedly."[16] Likewise, in <u>Sertorious and Eumenes Compared</u> it is said of Eumenes that he was "willing to live after being taken prisoner, neither took precautions against death, nor faced it well, but supplicating and entreating the foe who was known to have power over his body only, he made him lord and master over the spirit also."[17]

Plutarch also used the word ψυχή in the sense of "a moral being" and he implies the necessary responsibility every man has for the welfare of his soul following physical death. Thus in speaking of the proper conception of judgement he says "the judge also must be naked and dead that he may view--the very soul of every man instantly after he had died, and isolated from all his kin, having left behind all earthly adornments, so that his judgement may be just."[18]

Plutarch also gives the word the sense of timelessness-- the idea of "the eternal soul." Plutarch thus indicates his belief in an immortal aspect of the human soul. This idea appears in such examples as "---the followers of Pythagoras declare that the spirit ψυχή of the dead cast no shadow---."[19] And again, "---death is, as it seems to be, nothing else than the severing

---

[16]<u>Plutarch's Lives</u>, Vol. XI, Aratus XIX.

[17]<u>Plutarch's Lives</u>, Vol. VIII, pp. 140.

[18]<u>Plutarch's Moralia</u>, Vol. II, 121c.

[19]<u>Plutarch's Moralia</u>, Vol. IV, 300c.

of two things, soul and body from each other."20 Thus in

Plutarch we have definite evidence of expansion of the concept

of the soul and indeed in Plutarch we have a view of the soul

which differs very little from current popular theological

notions.

Plutarch also views ψυχή   as having a fondness for

learning and seeing. In Brutus S. 37, Brutus tells Cassius of

an apparition he had seen.

> Cassius who belonged to the school of Epicurus and
> was in the habit of taking issues on such topics with
> Brutus, said, This is our doctrine, Brutus, that we do
> not really feel or see everything but perception by the
> senses is a pliant and deceitful thing, and besides, the
> intelligence is very keen to change and transfor the
> thing perceived into any and every shape from one which
> has no real existence. An impression on the senses is
> like wax, and the soul (ψυχή   ) of man, in which the
> plastic material and the plastic power alike exist, can
> very easily shape and embellish it at pleasure.21

Summary

1. Herodotus felt that the first occurrence of the

concept of soul as something separate from, and yet closely

related to the physical body was among the Egyptians.

2. The earliest use of the word ψυχή was to indicate

the animating force which resides in the human body and which

is expressed in the breath and in the movement of respiration.

3. As early as Homer the ψυχή was used to indicate

the life of an individual.

4. For Homer the ψυχή was specifically human and went

20Plutarch's Moralia, Vol. II, 121E.

21Plutarch's Lives, Vol. VI, pp. 206-209.

to the underworld after the death of the body. From there it could sometimes emerge in manifestation to those who were alive.

5.   The concept of ψυχή continued to expand and gradually became an omnibus term for a man's total psychological functioning.

6.   The concept of the disparate soul which could exist separately from the body gradually became firmly established in Homeric thought.

7.   Pythagoras taught that since everything in the universe is eternal souls must also pre-exist and be subject to transmigration.

8.   Socrates expounded the classical Greek concept of the soul as a separate immaterial entity which was capable of existence apart from the body.

9.   Philo frequently used the word ψυχή to mean "earthly life" and also to indicate the total person.

10.   Philo also spoke of the separation of the soul from the body.

11.   Plutarch used the word ψυχή psychologically, for the seat of affective experience and also for the notion of man as "a moral being."

12.   Plutarch also gave the word ψυχή a sense of time-lessness which was in accord with his notion of "an immortal soul."

Chapter X

SOUL IN THE HEBREW OLD TESTAMENT, THE SEPTUAGINT
AND INTER-TESTAMENTAL LITERATURE

Soul in the Hebrew Old Testament

In most instances the word "soul" in the King James
Version is the translation of the Hebrew word   נֶפֶשׁ . Like
the English word soul, the Hebrew word   נֶפֶשׁ has a variety
of meanings which can be only understood by a thorough examination
of its usage.

Froom[1] has given an excellent summary of the use of
נֶפֶשׁ   in the Old Testament.

1. נֶפֶשׁ   Has Several Common Meanings. - The
Hebrew word   נֶפֶשׁ   like the English word "soul," has more
than one meaning, some being not synonymous with the English
meanings of "soul."

Koehler and Baumgartner in their lexicon give the
following meanings for   נֶפֶשׁ   :

1. Throat.

2. Breath, the breathing substance, making man and
animal living beings; the soul (strictly distinct from the Greek
notion of soul), the seat of which is in the blood.

3. Living being.

---

[1]L. Edwin Froom, The Conditionalist Faith of our Fathers,
Vol. I, p. 146.

4.   Soul as equal to living being, individual, person.

5.   Breath, soul, personality.

6.   Breath as equal to life.

7.   Breath as equal to soul as the seat of moods, emotions, and passions.[2]

Similiar to this is the general classification of the various usages of נֶפֶשׁ adopted by Bullinger[3] in his lexicon:

1.   "CREATURE" - "beast," "thing."

2.   "PERSON" - "man," "men," "him," "me," "yourselves," "himself," "we," "he," "myself," "her," "thee," "herself," "thyself," "themselves," "dead," "body," "one," "any," "they," "own," "fellow," "deadly," "mortally," "soul."

3.   "LIFE" and "LIVES" - "ghost," "breath."

4.   "DESIRE" - "mind," "heart," "lust," "pleasure," "discontented," "will," "greedy," "hearty," "appetite."

II.   A General Definition of נֶפֶשׁ - With this much before us, perhaps it is appropriate to attempt a definition of נֶפֶשׁ . As a start, at least, we can quote a modern book that is the combined work of many scholars "with a thorough knowledge of modern scholarship and theology," to quote the jacket-flap description of the book. Here is the definition:

> SOUL (נֶפֶשׁ) means the living being. We might render it "person" or "personality," so long as we remember that in Heb. thought even an animal is a נֶפֶשׁ . In passages of dignified or poetic diction the word is used

---

[2]Lexicon in Veteris Testamenti Libros, Ludwig Koehler and Walter Baumgartner, eds., vol. 2, pp. 626, 627.

[3]E. W. Bullinger, A Critical Lexicon and Concordance, p. 721.

instead of the personal pronoun (my soul-I or me); or to give a reflexive sense (his soul-himself, etc.). Roughly speaking, it means mind as distinct from matter (to quote the terminology of a once familiar dualism), but always includes more than mind in the limited sense of the reasoning faculty. It includes feelings, interest, and inclination; cf. Jer. 15:1.[4]

III. Basic Idea That of Individual Himself. – נֶפֶשׁ comes from the root נָפַשׁ , a verb used three times in the Old Testament (Ex. 23:12; 31:17; 2 Sam. 16: 14), in each case with the meaning "to revive oneself" or "to refresh oneself." The verb seems to go back to the basic meaning of breathing, and in the three times it is used the ordinary English reader might be tempted to translate it colloquially as "catch one's breath" or "take a breather," as after some extreme physical exertion.

נֶפֶשׁ as meaning the individual himself, is best illustrated by the portrayal of man's creation. As translated from the Hebrew in the R.S.V., it reads: "The Lord God formed man of dust from the ground, and breathed into his nostrils the breath of life; and man became a living being; (Gen. 2:7). Since each person is a distinct unit of life, the uniqueness of individuality seems to be the idea emphasized in the Hebrew word נֶפֶשׁ . And since the obvious evidence of life is breath and breathing, it is easy to understand how נֶפֶשׁ is used of man as a living being. Thus the R.S.V. translation is an accurate rendering of the Hebrew word.

נֶפֶשׁ is also used of animals, and is appropriately

---

[4]A Theological Word Book of the Bible, Alan Richardson, ed., art. "Mind, Heart," p. 144.

rendered "creature" in both the K.J.V. and R.S.V. Since animals

breathe as evidence of life, the Hebrew use of the word here

seems appropriate. As a matter of fact, animals are called

נֶפֶשׁ חַיָּה ("living creatures," K.J.V.) in Genesis 1.

The basic idea that נֶפֶשׁ is the individual himself,

rather than merely a constitutent part of the individual, seems

to underlie the various usages of נֶפֶשׁ . From this basic

idea springs the idiomatic use of נֶפֶשׁ for the personal pronoun

- "my soul" for "I" and "me"; "thy soul" for "you," etc.,

to use the common English translations in the Bible.

The majority of the occurrences of נֶפֶשׁ may be properly

translated by "person," "individual," "life," or by the appro-

priate personal pronoun.

There are also a substantial number of places in the

Bible where נֶפֶשׁ applies to the inner being, if by this term

we will understand, נֶפֶשׁ as the seat of mind, heart, emotions,

will.

Another useful analysis is to be found in the <u>Companion</u>

<u>Bible</u>.[5]

נֶפֶשׁ occurs in the Old Testament 754 times. In

the K.J.V. and the R.V. it is translated "soul" 472 times, and

by 44 different words in 282 other occurrences.

נֶפֶשׁ is used of the lower animals only - in 22

instances. נֶפֶשׁ is used of lower animals and man - 7 times.

(The first usage of נֶפֶשׁ is Genesis 1:20).

---

[5]E. W. Bullinger (Ed.) <u>The Companion Bible</u>, Appendix
13, p. 19.

נֶפֶשׁ is used of man as an individual - 53 times.

נֶפֶשׁ is used of man as exercising certain powers or performing certain acts - 96 times.

נֶפֶשׁ is used of man as possessing animal appetites and passions - 22 times.

נֶפֶשׁ is used of man as exercising mental faculties and manifesting feelings, affections, and passions - 231 times in 20 different ways.

נֶפֶשׁ is used of man "cut off" by God, and being slain or killed - in 54 passages.

נֶפֶשׁ is used of man as mortal, subject to death, but from which he can be delivered - in 243 passages.

נֶפֶשׁ is used of man as actually dead - in 13 passages.

Finally, נֶפֶשׁ is used of man (all rendered "soul") as going (1) to sheol, (2) to the "grave," (3) to "hell," (4) to the "pit"-hence a grave, (5) a "deep pit," and (6) into "silence."

An examination of the references to the occurrences of נֶפֶשׁ in Young's analytical and Strong's exhaustive concordance reveals the following figures.

"In the K.J.V. the Hebrew word נֶפֶשׁ is translated as follows:

471 times soul (every text in the Old Testament where soul is used except two, Job 30:15 and Isa. 57:16).

118 times life (Life's, lives).

29 times person.

15 times mind.

15 times heart.

9 times creature.

7 times body.

5 times dead.

4 times man.

3 times me.

3 times beast.

2 times ghost.

1 time fish.

נֶפֶשׁ is also translated one or more times as we, he, thee, they, her, herself, him (and other forms of the personal pronoun), and as will, appetite, lust, thing, breath, etc."

It is therefore clear that the meaning of נֶפֶשׁ can only be obtained by a close examination of its usage throughout the Old Testament. Such a study, in addition, leads to a number of conclusions.

(1) נֶפֶשׁ is not an independent entity-something that is separate, or separable, from the individual himself; something put into one when he is brought into being, and that lives on after he is dead, a sort of double, another self. There are not two personalities in man. Man is an integer, a single personality, a unit.

(2) נֶפֶשׁ does not denote something peculiar to man alone, distinguishing him from the animals beneath him in the scale of being. There is assuredly a radical difference, a fixed gulf, between the lowest type of man and the very highest order or brute or beast. But נֶפֶשׁ is not the differentiating factor, for the term נֶפֶשׁ is applied to lower animals as

well as man.

(3) נֶפֶשׁ definitely does not designate something
in man that is immortal and indestructible.[6]

נֶפֶשׁ and ψυχή in Palestinian Judaism

Consistent with Old Testament usage, the Hebrew post-
biblical works consider נֶפֶשׁ to be the vital principle of
life in man. Under the Hellenistic influence, however, the
Rabbis soon became attracted to a Greek anthropology which was
markedly different from that contained in the Hebrew Scriptures.
In contrast to the Old Testament view that the soul of a man
is a manifestation of the life given to the body by נֶפֶשׁ are
the views of Rabbi Simai who writes that, "All creatures which
were made from heaven, whose soul and body is from heaven and
his body is from earth."[7]

The soul which comes from heaven is likened to a guest
of the body which gives heavenly strength to its host. The
pagan Greek ideas of the immortality of the soul as a disparate
entity were not only absorbed but expanded as may be noted in
the statements of the Tamaites and Amoraeans. Thus the soul now
not only has a heavenly origin but resided with God before the
creation of the world, a decidely platonic notion. At death the
soul leaves the body as a distinct entity but returns to it at

[6]Edwin L. Froom, The Conditionalist Faith of our Fathers,
p. 152.

[7]Kittel, Theological Dictionary of the New Testament,
Vol. IX, p. 636.

the moment of resurrection.

Soul in the Septuagint and Inter-Testamental Works

As we have seen the word for soul in the Old Testament is the Hebrew word נֶפֶשׁ which literally means "that which breathes." This is the word which is consistently rendered by ψυχή in the Septuagint and in over 95 percent of the occurrences of ψυχή , it occurs as a translation of the Hebrew word נֶפֶשׁ. Occasionally another Hebrew word is found which ψυχή translates, but these instances are rare and for our purposes unimportant.

ψυχή

ψυχή is used in the Old Testament to communicate a number of ideas.

(1) To indicate the man himself;

(2) Instead of personal pronouns; (Gen. 49:6; Isa. 43:4)

(3) Instead of reflexive pronouns; (Job 9:21; I Sam. 20:17)

(4) To indicate the seat of the physical appetites;

(5) To indicate the source of affect. (I Kings 11:37)

In this connection the ψυχή requires Ego control whether volitional or unconscious and is also the root of chronic hostility and bitterness.

(6) Used with καρδία it includes the idea of intellect and conation as well as affect. (Deut. 4:29; 2 Kings 23:26).

ψυχή in the Apocalyptic and Pseud-Epigraphical Works

The notion of the soul as a separate immaterial and invisible entity, which is so foreign to the Hebrew concept of נֶפֶשׁ , is, however, the common one in the vast majority of the non-canonical writings. Thus at death the soul departs from the body and returns to God or goes to the underworld. After death then comes some type of judgement or retribution. This, however, applies only to the souls of men and not to animals. The souls of animals, however, have a special place of residence and are kept there to act as witnesses for the prosecution in the judgement.[8] The soul of man is said to reunite with the body for the judgement. A distinction is also noted between the Old Testament in that on calling up the dead it is now the soul which is said to appear. This is in marked contrast to the case of the witch of Endor (I Sam. 28:14ff).

The notion of the soul as a separate entity capable of existence apart from the body continued to be accepted and indeed elaborated upon in later Jewish thinking.

> How widespread is the idea that the body and soul
> are twofold may be seen from the fact that, directly
> or indirectly, under the influence of philosophical
> anthropology, thought is given to the distribution of
> the functions of the soul to members of the body, ----
> as also to the ensouling of the embryo,--------As things
> now stand we cannot say for certain what is the common
> origin of the common separation of body and soul in
> Judaism.[9]

ψυχή in Wisdom

The notion of ψυχή in Wisdom is wholly Greek with the by now established body/soul antithesis. The body is a mere burden which the soul or its νοῦς or λογισμός must tolerate. The soul continues to live on in the hereafter and

---

[8]Kittel, _Theological Dictionary of the New Testament_, Vol. IX, p. 633.

[9]Kittel, _Theological Dictionary of the New Testament_, Vol. IX, p. 633.

to receive rewards and punishments. Man, as the image of his creator, is considered to have innate immortality.

Summary

1. נֶפֶשׁ occurs 752 times in the Old Testament and is sometimes used in a purely physical sense with reference to the neck.

2. Since the basic idea of life in Hebrew thought was movement, נֶפֶשׁ came to represent vitality, the movement of that which is alive. Animals share the characteristics with man and are thus called "living souls" (Genesis 1:20-24).

3. נֶפֶשׁ is used to indicate the life-principle (Genesis 36:21).

4. נֶפֶשׁ is used to denote the physical vitality of an individual (Numbers 11:6).

5. נֶפֶשׁ is used to indicate affective functioning. (Job 3:16).

6. נֶפֶשׁ is used to denote conative functioning. (Genesis 23:8).

7. The word נֶפֶשׁ is the equivalent of the Greek ψυχή .

8. נֶפֶשׁ always includes נְשָׁמָה but is not limited to it. In I Kings 17:7 lack of נְשָׁמָה causes the departure of נֶפֶשׁ which returns when the prophet gives the child breath again, for נֶפֶשׁ alone is what makes a living creature into a living organism.

9. When breath and blood leave the body, then every form of life disappears. In Lev. 17:11, the seat of the נֶפֶשׁ

is considered to be in the blood and thus blood is only effective as an atoning agent so long as the vital force of נֶפֶשׁ is in it. In this connection blood simply means "life-force."

10. נֶפֶשׁ is the usual term for man's total nature, for what he is and not just what he has.

11. The נֶפֶשׁ is almost always connected with a form. It has no separate existence apart from the body. Hence the best translation is in many instances "person" as comprised in corporeal reality.

12. Each individual is a נֶפֶשׁ and when the texts speak of a single נֶפֶשׁ for a totality, the totality is viewed as a single person, a "corporate personality."

13. Hence the נֶפֶשׁ can denote what is most individual in human nature, namely, the ego, and it can become a synonym or the personal pronoun. Genesis 27:25.

14. According to the Old Testament the נֶפֶשׁ has no existence apart from the individual who possesses it, or, better, who is it. It never leaves him to pursue an independent life of its own.

15. The נֶפֶשׁ is never a force outside the individual that works variously in life and death.

16. The inhabitants of Sheol are never called נֶפֶשׁ. Because the emphasis is on the person it became permissible to use the term for the lifeless corpse (Numbers 6:6, 19:13, Lev. 19:28, 22:4) as long as the corpse still retained its distinguishing features and had not yet decomposed.

17. Since it is the נֶפֶשׁ which gives life to the total body as well as to its various parts, by the figure of

metyomy נֶפֶשׁ came to be used as a synonym for these various parts.

18. In post biblical Hebrew writers continue to use נֶפֶשׁ as the vital principle but gradually they were more and more attracted to a Hellenistic anthropology.

19. In the LXX the word ψυχή is used for the total man as well as pronominally and to indicate psychological functions.

20. In the inter-Testamental and apocalytic Greek works the concept of ψυχή is foreign to the Hebrew concept of נֶפֶשׁ and is rather classically Platonic.

Chapter XI

ψυχή IN THE NEW TESTAMENT, IN JOSEPHUS
AND IN THE PAPYRI

ψυχή in the New Testament

In the New Testament there are a number of distinct
uses of ψυχή . ψυχή , being derived from a verb
which means "to breath," has the same basic meaning as נֶפֶשׁ.
It is used in the New Testament 105 times and is used to indicate
the totality of man, his spiritual, physical and psychological
life, all combined into a single functioning unit. Thus in
the New Testament on 50 occasions ψυχή is translated
"soul," 40 times as "physical life" and 5 times as "mind" or
"heart," that is, psychological functioning.

Close examination of the occurrence of ψυχή in the
New Testament reveals that it is used in four distinct senses.

1. It is used in the sense of physical or natural
life. Eg. "they are dead which sought the young child's life
(ψυχή) (Matthew 2:20). Often the idea of self sacrifice is
prominent as when the good shepherd lays down his life ψυχή
for the sheep. (Jn. 10:11). Similarly, although, making only
infrequent use of ψυχή , Paul does use it in the sense of
physical life. (Phil. 2:30). "Because, for the work of Christ,
he was near unto death, not regarding his life, to supply your
lack of service toward me."

128

2. The word ψυχή is also used to indicate the self, man as a psychological unit, the personality or as man "in function." Thus the word came to be synonymous with the personal pronoun as can be seen by comparing Matthew 16:26 with Luke 9:25 where ψυχή is seen to be equated with ἑαυτον. Similarly in Acts 2:41 many souls ψυχή were added to the church, namely, many "total-individuals" were saved.

Hort has summarized this use of ψυχή as follows:

> ψυχή is in both Testaments first the individual being or his or its individual life (Genesis 1:20, 2:7), and then by a natural transition whatever is felt to belong most essentially to man's life when his bodily life has come to be recognized as a secondary thing. It answers very nearly to our modern word and conception "self"; and it is curious how often its force is well brought out by substituting "self" as a paraphrase------ It is the nexus in which all powers find their unit, that which is at once most individual and most permanent in us.[1]

3. ψυχή is also the source of all of the affective life of man. Thus the ψυχή is the source of love for God (Luke 12:27) "Consider the lilies how they grow. They toil not, they spin not; and yet I say unto you that Solomon, in all his glory, was not arrayed like one of these."; of sorrow (Matthew 26:38) "Then saith he unto them, My soul is exceedingly sorrowful, even unto death; tarry here, and watch with me."; of desire (Revelation 18:14) "And the fruits that thy soul lusted after are departed from thee, and all things which were dainty and sumptuous are departed from thee, and thou shalt find them no more at all."; and of fear (Acts 2:43) "And fear came upon every

---

[1] F. J. A. Hort, Commentary on I Peter, p. 134.

soul; and many wonders and signs were done by the apostles."

4.   ψυχή   is also used to emphasize the higher or
spiritual side of man as compared with the desire of his lower
or animal nature. It is this double use of the word which
underlies the saying of Christ in Matthew 16:25. "Whosoever
would save his   ψυχή   will loose it; and whosoever looses his
ψυχή   for my sake will find it." Similarly we are encour-
aged by the fact that even though there are those who may kill
the body they are not able to kill the   ψυχή   , namely,
the higher or spiritual aspect of man. The "higher-nature" of
man cannot, on the basis of the scriptural use of the word, be
equated with an extra-corporeal metaphysical appendage. It
appears to be rather the sum total of a man's life with a special
emphasis on that which is oriented to God, an experience of
purpose, meaning and a sense of values.

Bullinger in his critical Lexicon gives a most excellent
summary of the uses of   ψυχή   in the Scriptures. The following
is a summary of his material.

ψυχή   , one of the manifestations of ζωή   (life),
viz. that which is manifested in animals, animal life;
hence, breath, (not breath as mere air, but as the sign
of life.) Once applied to vegetable life, Is. x. 18.

In O.T. everywhere LXX. for   נפש   and is said to
be possessed by all the lower creatures, Gen. i. 20,21,24,
30; ii. 7,19; ix. 10,12,15,16; Lev. xi. 10,46; Numb. xxxi,
28; Prov. vii. 23; xii. 10; Ezek. xlvii, 9. See also,
Rev. xiii. 9; xvi. 3.

It denotes the vital principle in animal bodies, 2
Ch. i. 11; 1 Sam. xxii, 23; 1 Kings i. 12; 2 Ch. i. 11;
Est. vii, 3; Prov. i, 19; vi. 26; xii. 10; Lam. ii. 19.
Also, Matt. xvi. 25,26; xx. 28; Luke xii. 19-23; 1 John
iii. 16.

It is used of the person as possessed of such life,

Gen. xii. 5; xiv, 21; xvii. 14; xix. 17,19,20; xlvi. 18;
Ex. xii. 15; Lev. iv. 2; v. 15; vii. 26; Est. ix. 31;
Is. xlvii. 14, (cf. Rev. vi. 9.). Also of a dead person,
(with the adj.) Lev. xxi. 11. And of those raised, Rev.
xx. 4, as contrasted with those yet unraised, Rev. xx. 5.

It can die or be killed, Lev. xxiv. 17,18; Judg. xvi.
30; Num. xxiii. 10; xxxi. 19; Deut. xix. 6; xxii. 26;
xxvii. 25; Prov. vii. 23; Ecc. iii. 19. So of persons,
Josh. x. 28, 30, 39; Lev. xxiii, 30. Also Matt. x. 28;
Mark iii. 4; Luke ix. 54-46; Rev. xvi. 3.

It goes to the grave, Job xxxiii. 22, and can be
hazarded by danger, Acts xv. 26; Rom. xi. 3.

It is identified with the blood, (as the Spirit never
is) Gen. ix. 4,5; Lev. xvii. 11,14; Ps. lxxii. 14; xciv.
21; Prov. xxviii. 17.

The Greek ψυχή is identified with Hebrew נֶפֶשׁ
by comparing Acts ii. 27 with Ps. xvi. 10; Rom. xi. 3
with 1 Kings xix. 10; 1 Cor. xv. 45 with Gen. ii. 7;
Matt. xx. 28 with Is. liii. 10.

"My soul" is the same as "me," or "myself," Num. xxiii.
10; Jud. xvi. 30; 1 Kings xx. 32; Ps. lix. 3; xxxv. 13;
cxxxi. 2; Jer. xviii. 20, (cf. xxxviii. 6.).

"His soul" is the same as "him" or "himself," Gen.
xxxvii. 21; Job xviii. 4; Ps. xx. 29; cv. 17, 18.[2]

In the New Testament the most common use of ψυχή

is for the total physical life and functioning of the individual

thus in Acts 20:10 Eutychus can be said to be alive because he

has ψυχή . Similarly in Acts 27:10 there is danger to the

ship and cargo and also to the ψυχή of the passengers.

The ψυχή can also indicate the psychological Ego and it

appears to be more intimately bound up with flesh and blood than

is ξωή.

Men may be influenced for good or for evil, (Acts 14:22)

---

[2]E. W. Bullinger, A Critical Lexicon and Concordance
to the English and Greek New Testament.

but it is ψυχή as the man himself which can be moved and influenced in this way. The idea of movement as an integral part of the decision-making process, viewed psychologically, appears to be basic to this use of ψυχή . The ψυχή may also be the locus of a variety of <u>affective</u> experiences in man. (Mk. 14:34).

Matthew 10:28 presents God as the one who can destroy both body and ψυχή in Gehenna. In this regard He is contrasted with man, who can kill the body alone but not the ψυχή. That God has power to cast into Hades and to take out of it is an Old Testament concept. Wisdom 16:13-15 also indicates that man can only kill but has no power over the πνεῦμα that has departed or the ψυχή that has been taken away. The Rabbis agreed that God can kill both in this aeon and in that which is to come. Even more precisely we find in 4 Macc. 13:13-15 a summons not to fear him who only seems to kill. God is the giver of ψυχαί and σώματα and there awaits evil-doers a more serious conflict of the ψυχή and the danger of eternal torment. The doctrine of the immortal soul is plainly intimated in this context. In Matthew 10:28, however, the reference to God's power to destroy the ψυχή and σῶμα in Hades is opposed to the idea of the immortality of the soul, for it is apparent that man can be thought of only as a whole, both ψυχή and σῶμα [3] In this connection it is noteworthy that Luke

---

[3]Kittel, <u>Theological Dictionary of the New Testament</u>, Vol. IX, pp. 645-646.

goes to great lengths to teach the corporeality of the resurrection as distinct from the Greek notion of the survival of
the soul.

ψυχή in Josephus

Josephus makes significant use of the word ψυχή
and uses it with the idea of "the force of mind." "I know no
fear great enough to drive this thought from my mind ψυχή." [4]
It also occurs with the meaning of "life": "for neither am
I better than my brothers, that I should spare my own life."[5]
Here, again, it is the total man which is in question.

ψυχή in the Papyri

The word ψυχή appears in the <u>Papyri</u> very frequently
and is there used with a variety of meanings. An example occurs
in a letter dated during the latter part of the second century
B.C. which states as follows: "Please therefore in the first
place give thanks to the gods and secondly to save many lives
ψυχή by seeking out in the neighborhood of your village
five arourae for our maintenance so that we may obtain food."[6]
The emphasis here appears to be on the purely physical life
which is sustained by food. The same idea occurs when the word
ψυχή is used to indicate life which may be cut out by
physical force.

---

[4] Joseph, <u>Antiquities</u>, Vol. XIII, 7.198.

[5] Joseph, <u>Antiquities</u>, Vol. XIII, 7.199.

[6] B. P. Grenfell, <u>The Tebtunis Papyri</u>, Vol. I, 56.11.

In the _Papyri_ the word soul is also used to indicate
the source of feelings and desires, i.e., the source of affect.
In this connection it appears to indicate the psychological
part of man as contrasted with his physical state. It is also
used to indicate the mental state of the individual and thus
is closely related to our idea of "mind." Thus mind is capable
of being upset: "he also persisted in vexing my soul ψυχή
about his slave."[7] The soul is also that part of man which is
related to reasoning and understanding and thus is the source
of his prayer requests: "turn to the Lord---He will not desert
you, but will fulfill the petitions of your soul ψυχή ."[8]
Up to this point the soul is always related to the idea of the
total man in function.

The _Papyri_, however, also develop the idea of the soul
as an immortal metaphysical entity separate and distinct from
the body. In this connection it is used to indicate that part
of the man which experiences eternity and thus indicates an
immortal part of man. Thus, not only is the word used in
conjunction with body and spirit, but it is used in association
with the idea of immortal life. In another reference to spiritual warfare use is made of the word ψυχή   to indicate
immortal souls which have departed from their bodies and thus
the soul is considered to be the part of man which continues to

---

[7]B. P. Grenfell, _The Oxyrhynchus Papyri_, Vol. VI,
903.33.

[8]Kirsopp Lake, _The Apostolic Fathers_, Vol. I, Mard.
8.9.2.

exist after death.[9] Again this is almost identical with current theological thinking.

Summary

1. ψυχή   in the New Testament means the physical life of man and also of animals.

2. ψυχή   in the New Testament is also the individual and personal life and never the phenomenon of life as such.

3. It can be used reflexively and pronominally and indicates man in toto.

4. It can be the seat of affective experience.

5. In the New Testament ψυχή   can never be surrendered from the physical life and is not identical with it.

ψυχή   is the life in its authenticity as given by God and as received from Him.

6. ψυχή   in the New Testament came to denote a life which is not ended by death. This is not, however, life maintained in some extra-somatic segment but in the life of faith continued eventually into resurrection life because of the faithfulness of God.

7. Like πνεῦμα ,   ψυχή   in the New Testament is not used to indicate the dead in some intermediate state. Paul is simply satisfied in knowing that the dead are with Christ.

8. Joseph uses ψυχή   to denote life and also the total man.

9. In the Papyri ψυχή   is used to indicate lives,

---

[9]B. P. Grenfell, The Oxyrhynchus Papyri, Vol. II, 1356.37.

physical life, affective experience, the mental state of an individual, the reasoning part of man, and also in the platonic sense of a separate immaterial entity capable of existence apart from the body.

Chapter XII

רוּחַ AND נְשָׁמָה IN THE OLD TESTAMENT AND
IN PALESTINIAN JUDAISM

The Use of רוּחַ in the Old Testament

The Hebrew word רוּחַ occurs some 380 times in the Old

Testament and in the vast majority of these occurrences it is

translated as "spirit," "wind," or "breath." When translated

"spirit" the word is found with a variety of meanings as will

be outlined below. The word is used of God some 90 times and

is also used to describe both good and bad angels. In 70

instances it is used to denote affective responses and attitudinal

styles such as anger, temper, and courage. It is used to denote

the life principle in man and in animals 25 times and 3 times

for the faculty of conation. In 16 instances it expresses moral

character.

As Froom says,

Since breath, wind, moral character, vitality, principle
of life, and spirit beings are all invisible, the underlying
idea of רוּחַ seems to suggest an invisible force, power,
or being, which acts to produce visible results.

We are dealing with man and his nature, and we may
therefore properly ignore all the uses of רוּחַ (spirit)
that refer to God and angels. We are interested in
breath as evidence of life, and in the principle of life
with which God has endowed man.[1]

There are six principal ways in which רוּחַ is used

_____

[1]L. Edwin Froom, The Conditionalist Faith of Our Fathers,
Vol. I, p. 152.

137

in the Old Testament. The following is a very small selection
of illustrative references.

I. To denote the third person of the Trinity, God
   the Holy Spirit.

   a. Job 33:4

   "The Spirit of God hath made me, and the breath
of the Almightly hath given me life."

   b. 1 Kings 18:12

   "And it shall come to pass, as soon as I am
gone from thee, that the Spirit of the Lord shall carry thee
where I know not; and so when I come and tell Ahab, and he cannot
find thee, he shall slay me. But I, thy servant, fear the Lord
from my youth."

   c. I Samuel 10:6

   "And the Spirit of the Lord will come upon thee,
and thou shalt prophesy with them, and shalt be turned into
another man."

   More specifically the Spirit is He who gives prophetic
powers and who is the divine energy behind the cherubim. (Ezek.
1:12; Ezek. 2:2). The Spirit is also said to be responsible for
ecstatic speech (Genesis 41:48); the author of the prophetic
message (Zech. 7:12, Num. 11:25); and the Spirit may lift up
and snatch away (2 Kings 18:12). The Spirit is also in a very
special manner associated with God's creative powers and operations
It is also noteworthy that God the Spirit may be associated with
man's spirit in the production of certain psychological abilities
and characteristics, such as insight, artistic sense, skill,

(Exodus 31:3) enlightenment, wisdom and perspicacity. (Daniel 5:14).

    II.   <u>For the wind as a physical phenomenon</u>.

       a.   <u>Exodus 14:21</u>

"And Moses stretched out his hand over the sea; and the Lord caused the sea to go back by a strong east <u>wind</u> all that night, and made the sea dry land, and the waters were divided.

       b.   <u>Genesis 3:8</u>

"And they heard the voice of the Lord God walking in the garden in the <u>cool</u> of the day: and Adam and his wife hid themselves from the presence of the Lord God among the trees of the garden."

       c.   <u>Zechariah 6:5</u>

"And the angel answered and said unto me, These are the four <u>spirits</u> of the heavens, which go forth from standing before the Lord of all the earth."

    III.   <u>For the wind as a symbol</u>.

       a.   <u>Job 6:26</u>

"Do ye imagine to reprove words, and the speeches of one that is desperate, which are as <u>wind</u>?"

       b.   <u>2 Kings 19:7</u>

"Behold, I will send a <u>blast</u> upon him, and he shall hear a rumor, and shall return to his own land; and I will cause him to fall by the sword in his own land."

The wind is an important emblem and symbol of the Holy Spirit. Girdlestone discusses at length the wind as a symbol of God in the Old Testament.

It is clear that the wind is regarded in scripture
as a fitting emblem of the mighty penetrating power
of the invisible God; and the breath is supposed to
symbolize, not only the deep feelings which are generated
within man, such as sorrow and anger, but also kindred
feelings in the divine nature. References in the Old
Testament to the Spirit of God and to the Spirit of the
Lord are more numerous than is sometimes imagined. In
upwards of twenty-five places, this divine Spirit is
spoken of entering man for the purpose of giving him
life, power, wisdom, or right feeling. God, moreover,
is called "The God of the spirits" in the New Testament;
and it is every where taught or implied that the personal
agency of God is in contact with the center of life in
every child of man. How he acts, we do not know; in
what mode he enlightens, inspires, comforts, and warns,
we cannot tell. We see and feel the results, but we
are unable to comprehend the processes.[2]

IV. <u>For the human breath, the product of inspiration</u>

<u>and expiration.</u>

a. <u>Job 19:17</u>

"My <u>breath</u> is strange to my wife, though I make

supplication to the children of mine own body."

b. <u>Job 9:18</u>

"He will not suffer me to take my <u>breath</u>, but

filleth me with bitterness."

V. <u>As a synonym for</u>

a. <u>The whole person - Ecclesiastes 1:17</u>

"And I gave my heart to know wisdom, and to

know madness and folly; I perceived that this also is vexation

of <u>spirit</u>."

b. <u>For life and living - Jeremiah 10:14</u>

"Every man is stupid in his knowledge; every

goldsmith is confounded by the engraved image; for his melted

---

[2]R. B. Girdlestone, <u>Synonyms of the Old Testament</u>, p. 60.

image is falsehood, and there is no breath in them."

Proverbs 25:28

"He that hath no rule over his own spirit is
like a city that is broken down, and without walls."

c. The total psychic apparatus - Psalms 32:2

"Blessed is the man unto whom the Lord imputeth
not iniquity, and in whose spirit there is no guile."

VI. For the life-principle in man and animals.

a. Ecclesiastes 3:19-21

"For that which befalleth the sons of men befalleth
them: as the one dieth, so dieth the other; yea, they have all
one breath, so that a man hath no pre-eminence above a beast;
for all is vanity."

"All go unto one place; all are of the dust, and
all turn to dust again."

"Who knoweth the spirit of man that goeth upward,
and the spirit of the beast that goeth downward to the earth?"

b. Ezekiel 37:5

"Thus saith the Lord God unto these bones, Behold,
I will cause breath to enter into you, and ye shall live."

c. Psalms 104:29

"Thou hidest thy face, they are troubled; thou
takest away their breath, they die, and return to their dust."

d. Ecclesiastes 12:7

"Then shall the dust return to the earth as it
was, and the spirit shall return unto God, who gave it."

e. Job 10:12

"Thou hast granted me life and favor, and thy care hath preserved my spirit."

VII.   As a technical psychological term.

a.   For the affect of depression.

1.   Genesis 26:35

"Who were a grief of mind unto Isaac and to Rebekah."

2.   I Samuel 1:15

"And Hannah answered and said, No, my Lord, I am a woman of a sorrowful spirit.   I have drunk neither wine nor strong drink, but have poured out my soul before the Lord."

3.   Proverbs 15:13

"A merry heart maketh a cheerful countenance, but by sorrow of the heart the spirit is broken."

4.   Isaiah 61:3

"To appoint unto those who mourn in Zion, to give unto them beauty for ashes, the oil of joy for mourning, the garment of praise for the spirit of heaviness, that they might be called trees of righteousness, the planting of the Lord, that he might be glorified."

5.   Exodus 6:9

"And Moses spoke so unto the children of Israel; but they hearkened not unto Moses for anguish of spirit, and for cruel bondage."

6.   Job 21:4

"As for me, is my complaint to man?   And if it were so, why should not my spirit be troubled?"

    b. <u>For the affect of hostility</u>.

      1. <u>Judges 8:3</u>

"God hath delivered into your hands the princes of Midian, Oreb and Zeeb: and what was I able to do in comparison with you? Then their <u>anger</u> was abated toward him, when he had said that."

    c. <u>For agitated depression</u>.

      1. <u>Job 6:4</u>

"For the arrows of the Almighty are within me, the poison of it drinketh up <u>my spirit</u>; the terrors of God do set themselves in array against me."

    d. <u>For jealousy</u>.

      1. <u>Numbers 5:14</u>

"And the <u>spirit</u> of jealousy come upon him, and he be jealous of his wife, and she be defiled: or if the <u>spirit</u> of Jealousy come upon him, and he be jealous of his wife, and she be not defiled;"

    e. <u>For cognition, and understanding</u>.

      1. <u>Job 32:8</u>

"But there is a <u>spirit</u> in man; and the inspiration of the Almighty giveth them understanding."

    f. <u>For Intellection</u>.

      1. <u>Daniel 6:3</u> (Chaldee)

"Then this Daniel was preferred above the presidents and princes, because an excellent <u>spirit</u> was in him; and the king thought to set him over the whole realm.

    g. <u>For the faculty of judgement and knowledge</u>.

1. Exodus 28:3

"And thou shalt speak unto all that are wise hearted, whom I have filled with the _spirit_ of wisdom, that they may make Aaron's garments to consecrate him, that he may minister unto me in the priest's office.

h. For confusion and ambivalence.

1. Isaiah 19:14

"The Lord hath mingled a _perverse spirit_ in the midst of it; and they have caused Egypt to err in every work of it, as a drunken man staggereth in his vomit."

i. For personality, and attudinal styles.

1. Determination and Courage - Joshua 2:11

"And as soon as we had heard these things, our hearts did melt, neither did there remain any more _courage_ in any man, because of you; for the Lord your God, he is God in heaven above, and in earth beneath."

2. Reliability - Proverbs 11:13

"A talebearer revealeth secrets, but he that is of a faithful _spirit_ concealeth the matter."

3. Religious orientation - Zechariah 12:10

"And I will pour upon the house of David, and upon the inhabitants of Jerusalem, the _spirit_ of grace and of supplications; and they shall look upon me whom they have pierced, and they shall mourn for him, as one mourneth for his only son, and shall be in bitterness for him, as one that is in bitterness for his firstborn."

4. Remorse and Willingness to Repent

Psalms 51:17

"The sacrifices of God are a broken spirit; a broken and a contrite heart, O God, thou wilt not despise."

j. Poor ego control and impulsivity.

Proverbs 16:32

"He who is slow to anger is better than the mighty; and he who ruleth his spirit, than he that taketh a city."

Ecclesiastes 7:9

"Be not hasty in thy spirit to be angry; for anger resteth in the bosom of fools."

k. Divinely stimulated intuition.

Daniel 4:8 (Chaldee)

"But at the last Daniel came in before me, whose name is Belteshazzar, according to the name of my god, and in whom is the spirit of the holy gods, and to him I told the dream, saying,..."

l. Specifically, for the ego.

Exodus 35:21

"And they came, everyone whose heart stirred him up, and everyone whom his spirit made willing, and they brought the Lord's offering to the work of the tabernacle of the congregation, and for all its service, and for the holy garments."

m. For cognitive processes becoming conscious.

Ezekiel 20:32

"And that which cometh into your mind shall

not be at all, that ye say, We will be as the nations, as the families of the countries, to serve wood and stone."

An interesting use of the word רוּחַ is found in Ecclesiastes 3:19 & 21. The text speaking of the sons of men and also of beasts indicates that a man has no pre-eminence above a beast because "all have one רוּחַ." The writer then asks the question "who knoweth the רוּחַ of man that goeth upward, and the רוּחַ of the beast that goeth downward to the earth?" In the Authorized Version the רוּחַ in verse 19 is translated "breath," whereas in verse 21 on both occasions it is translated "spirit." "For that which befalleth the sons of men befalleth beasts. Even one thing befalleth them: as the one dieth, so dieth the other; yea, they have all one breath, so that a man hath no pre-eminence above a beast; for all is vanity. All go unto one place; all are of the dust, and all turn to dust again. Who knoweth the spirit of man that goeth upward, and the spirit of the beast that goeth downward to the earth?"

Undoubtedly, it is translated spirit in verse 21 because of the phrase, speaking of man, that he "goeth upward." This translation would seem to be without real justification. Contextually the word should be translated the same in both passages and if in verse 19 it is indicated that man and animals have "one breath" then verse 21 should read "who knoweth the breath of man that goeth upward, and the breath of the beast that goeth downward to the earth?"

Rather than this having reference to the upward flight of the spirit or the soul of the man and the opposite for the

beast it would seem more reasonable to interpret the verse as
having reference to the general position of the head of the man
versus the position of the head of the beast during inspiration
and expiration. Man tends to breathe with the face turned more
or less horizontally to upwards while typically the beast breathes
downwards towards the earth.

An examination of all the usages of רוּחַ in the Old
Testament makes it very clear that the רוּחַ as the life-principle in man is never said to possess a separate conscience
existence in itself. It is always seen to be given to man at
the beginning of his existence and to be withdrawn at the moment
of death. When God withdraws the life-principle from man he
is powerless to maintain a hold on life. "There is no man that
hath power over the spirit רוּחַ to retain the spirit רוּחַ;
neither hath he power in the day of death." (Eccl. 8:8).

There is one occurrence of רוּחַ which may appear
on initial examination to be somewhat different from other
meanings. Numbers 16:22 reads as follows: "And they fell upon
their faces, and said, O God, the God of the spirit רוּחַ
of all flesh, shall one man sin, and wilt thou be wroth with
the whole congregation." A similar use is found in Numbers 27:16.
The new Jewish Publication Society Torah renders Numbers 16:22
as, "O God, Source of the breath of all flesh." This must be
considered as the preferable and accurate rendering since it
is consistent with the use of the word elsewhere in the Old
Testament.

Bullinger[3] has provided an excellent summary of the uses of רוּחַ He says that:

> The meaning of the word is to be deduced only from its usage. The one root idea running through all the passages is <u>invisible force</u>. As this force may be exerted in varying forms, and may be manifested in diverse ways, so various rendering are necessitated, corresponding thereto.
>
> רוּחַ , in whatever sense it is used, always represents that which is invisible except by its manifestations. These are seen both externally to man, as well as internally within man.
>
> As coming from God, it is the invisible origin of life. All apart from this is death. It comes from God, and returns to God. (Eccl. 3:19-20). Hence, רוּחַ is used of

I.   God, as being invisible "The spirit of Jehovah" is Jehovah himself, in His manifestation of invisible power.

II.   The Holy Spirit: The Third person of the Trinity.

III.   Invisible Divine power manifesting itself.

  Increation
  In giving life
  In executing judgement -
   "beast"
   "breath"

IV.   Invisible "Power from on High," manifesting itself as Divine power in giving spiritual gifts. Spoken of as coming upon, clothing, falling on, and being poured out. Rendered "Spirit," but should be "spirit."

V.   The invisible part of man (psychological) given by God at man's formation at birth, and returning to God at his death.

VI.   The invisible characteristics of man; manifesting themselves in states of mind and feeling (by the Figure of Metonymy)

  "Mind"
  "Breath"

---

[3]E. W. Bullinger, <u>Companion Bible</u>, Appendix 9, p. 13.

"Courage"
"Anger"
"Blast"
"Spirit"

VII.   Put by the Figure Synecdoche for the whole person.

VIII.   Invisible spirit beings.

"Angels"
"Cherubim"
"Neutral Spirit-Beings"
"Evil Angels"

IX.   The invisible manifestations of the atmosphere.

"Temperature"
"Air"
"Wind"

It is also important to note that the spirit in man is distinct from the life which it produces as the cause is different from the effect. As Froom[4] has so accurately stated:

> This differentiation is highly important. If the life of man were identical with the spirit that produced it, it would possess all the essential attributes of the spirit. But this is safe-guarded in the Scripture account, which describes the spirit as the cause of life, but distinct and distinguishable from it. Thus the effect may perish, but the cause does not perish. The life of man may disappear and become extinct, while the spirit, or breath, from the Almighty does not. It simply returns to Him from whom it came.
>
> Man has the breath, or spirit, of God within him. But the spirit may be withdrawn, since it is only a loan from God for the duration of man's lifetime. Job significantly describes life as "all the while my breath (neshamah) is in me, and the spirit (ruach) of God is in my nostrils"(Job 27:3). Job knew that his spirit, or breath, was not his own, with an independent and innate right to keep it, but was the spirit, or breath, of God in his nostrils - subject to withdrawal at his Maker's will. Job recognized himself as intrinsically but "dust" (Job 10:9;34:15).

---

[4]L. Edwin Froom, The Conditionalist Faith of Our Fathers, Vol. I, p. 156.

נְשָׁמָה in the Old Testament

In the Old Testament the word נְשָׁמָה is found as a synonym for the word רוּחַ . It is the word נְשָׁמָה which is used in the account of the creation of man in Genesis 2:7. נְשָׁמָה is not a common word and is found only infrequently in the Old Testament and with a variety of meanings.

Breath	17 times
Blast	3 times
Spirit	2 times
Souls	Once
Inspiration	Once

These translations are as indicated in the following outline.

1. Breath - 13 times

Genesis 2:7

"And the Lord God formed man of the dust of the ground, and breathed into his nostrils the breath of life; and man became a living soul."

2. To breathe - 4 times

1 Kings 15:29

"And it came to pass, when he reigned, that he smote all the house of Jeroboam; he left not to Jeroboam any who breathed, until he had destroyed him, according unto the saying of the Lord, which he spoke by his servant, Ahijah, the Shilonite."

3. Blast - 3 times

2 Samuel 22:16

"And the channels of the sea appeared; the foun-
dations of the world were laid bare, at the rebuking of the
Lord, at the <u>blast</u> of the breath of his nostrils."

    4. <u>Spirit</u> - 2 times

    <u>Proverbs 20:27</u>

"The <u>spirit</u> of man is the lamp of the Lord,
searching all the inward parts."

    5. <u>Inspiration</u> - 1 time

    <u>Job 32:8</u>

"But there is a spirit in man; and the <u>inspiration</u>
of the Almighty giveth them understanding."

    6. <u>Soul</u> - 1 time

    <u>Isaiah 57:16</u>

"For I will not contend forever, neither will I
be always angry; for the spirit should fail before me, and the
<u>souls</u> which I have made."

נְשָׁמָה   and   רוּחַ   are also found in a number of
instances of poetic parallelism in the Old Testament.

    I. "By the blast   נְשָׁמָה   of God they perish, and
by the breath רוּחַ   of his nostrils are they consumed."
(Job 4:9)

    II. "All the while my breath   נְשָׁמָה   is in me, and
the spirit   רוּחַ   of God is in my nostrils."   (Job 27:3).

    III. "But there is a spirit   רוּחַ   in man: and the
inspiration   נְשָׁמָה   of the Almighty giveth them understanding."
(Job 32:8)

    IV. "The Spirit of the Lord   רוּחַ   hath made me,
and the breath   נְשָׁמָה   of the Almighty hath given me life."

(Job 33:4).

V. "If he sets his heart upon man, if he gather unto himself his spirit רוּחַ and his breath נְשָׁמָה ; all flesh shall perish together, and many shall turn again into dust." (Job 34:14-15).

VI. "He that giveth breath נְשָׁמָה unto the people upon it, and Spirit רוּחַ to them that walk therein." (Isaiah 42:5).

Spirit in Palestinian Judaism

As in the Old Testament so in later Hebrew and Aramaic רוּחַ is the usual word for wind. Beings from the heavenly world, such as angels, are also called "spirits." Later Jewish anthropology developed the idea that the רוּחַ may represent the dead man in the grave and other mythologic notions which went far beyond the use of the word in the Old Testament proper. It departed from the Old Testament view and eventually developed a distinction between spirit and body so that there arose a dualistic anthropology with a belief in the pre-existence and immortality of the soul as a separate anthropological entity. Thus, quite early in Hellenistic Judaism the idea of the life of the spirit, as a separate personal entity, after death was attested. The notion that the spirit of the righteous dead experiences joy after death while the bones remained at peace in the dust, was the outcome. It is thus clear that the anthropology of Hellenistic Judaism developed under the influence of Hellenistic ideas and concepts, which is to be expected since Palestinian Judaism did not exist on an island but was undoubtedly influenced by the Greek culture which surrounded it.

This period of Palestinian Judaism covers the two centuries immediately prior to the Christian era and it is clear that in this period the Jews absorbed the basic elements of Platonic pagan philosophy concerning man, his constitution and destiny. When they did this they clearly departed from the inspired teaching of the writers of the Old Testament although a few remained true to the teaching of revelation.

With the close of the line of the Old Testament prophets there came the period of the priests and a number of different sects emerged. Firstly, there was the group of Pharisees who were formalists and traditionalists. They were the religious leaders. Secondly there was the group of the Sadducees who were materialists and skeptics and they openly disavowed the Pharisaic notion of disembodied spirits and souls and especially the resurrection. The Pharisees and Sadducees were in constant conflict in the Inter-Testamental and early New Testament periods. The Sadducees remained the minority party and disappeared with the destruction of Jerusalem. The Pharisees were thus left to develop and impose their concepts and to produce the legalistic literature of Judaism, namely the Mishnah (Circa 200 A.D.) and the Talmud (Circa 200-500 A.D.) and to promulgate their platonic views of man.

It was also during this Inter-Testamental period and in response to such chronic conflicts that the Aprocrypha was produced and it was to prove to be a combination of fact and fanciful fiction. In particular, these books were Apocalyptic

in orientation being produced by a variety of mystics and seers.
One of the major issues in these works was the question of
eschatology and thus the nature of soul, spirit, and the
resurrection life of man became a major focus of examination.

In order to support a wide variety of such notions and
speculations a number of writers used the pen names of various
former Jewish prophets as pen names. This was done to increase
the prestige, acceptance and credibility of the works and so
there came into existence such works as the <u>Book of Enoch</u>, the
<u>Testaments of the Twelve Patriarchs</u>, the <u>Wisdom of Solomon</u>,
the <u>Assumption of Moses</u>, etc. These books were therefore called
the pseudoepigraphical writings and although of doubtful author-
ship and date they offer clear evidence of the absorption of
Platonic ideas and notions by Jewish thinking. It is also
worthy of note that these works were highly influenced by the
concepts of the nations surrounding Palestine such as the Egyptians, Babylonians, Persians, but especially by the Greeks to
whom the Jews had been subject in a succession of captivities.
Thus the development of רוּחַ in the Inter-Testamental period
was closely associated with that of נֶפֶשׁ and was subject
to the same influences.

Summary

1. רוּחַ is used very frequently in the Old Testament and is most often translated, "spirit," "wind" or "breath."

2. The underlying idea of רוּחַ appears to be that
of invisible force which acts to produce visible results.

3. רוּחַ is used to indicate the three members of

the God-head.

4. It is also used for wind as a physical phenomenon as well as for wind as a symbol.

5. It is used to indicate the whole man as well as a variety of aspects of psychological functioning.

6. It is used to denote the life-principle in both man and animals.

7. רוּחַ as the life-principle in man is never said to possess a separate conscience existence in itself.

8. רוּחַ is given to men at the beginning of their existence and returns to God at the moment of death.

9. רוּחַ is used to indicate a variety of invisible spirit beings.

10. The רוּחַ in man is distinct from the life which it produces.

11. In the Inter-Testamental period רוּחַ became associated with a dualistic Hellenistic anthropology with a belief in the pre-existence and immortality of the soul as a separate entity.

12. In the Old Testament נְשָׁמָה is found as a synonym for רוּחַ although רוּחַ is wider in scope.

13. נְשָׁמָה is translated breath, blast, spirit, inspiration and soul on one occasion.

14. נְשָׁמָה and רוּחַ are used as counterparts in poetic parallelism in many instances.

Chapter XIII

πνεῦμα   IN SECULAR GREEK AND IN HELLENISTIC JUDAISM

The Meaning of πνεῦμα Developmentally in Secular Greek

The word πνεῦμα orginally conveyed the notion of wind
and nothing more, and in the Old Testament the only word used
to denote wind is the Hebrew word for πνεῦμα , namely, רוּחַ.
The earliest Greek word used for wind was πνοή   and, indeed,
this is the only word used by Homer for this purpose. From the
time of Herodotus it is the word πνεῦμα   which came to be
the common word for wind. Since the movements of inspiration
and expiration produce air in motion πνεῦμα   , very naturally,
next came to connote the idea of breath. Breathing, however, is
intimately associated with and most often recognized by movement so πνεῦμα   soon took on the meaning of vital movement or
life. It was then but a small step for πνεῦμα   to come to
be used of the principle of life itself. It is thus used in
Aeschylus Pers. 507, in Euripides Phoencia 851.[1] Similarly it
is used to denote the principle of life in Polybius, Plutarch
and numerous other later Greek authors. It is also interesting
to note that in Sophocles FR. 13. man is said to be "πνεῦμα καὶ
σκία."   This may be an early precursor of the dichotomous

_____

[1]Kittel, Theological Dictionary of the New Testament,
Vol. VI, p. 336.

view of the structure of man.

The πνεῦμα is considered to be the principle or energy of life which does not come from man (2 Macc. 7:22) but from God. (Job 27:3). God sends it, controls it and withdraws it (Daniel 5:4 LXX, Job 3:6) and this results in man's death. (Bar. 2:17, Sir. 38:23). Man has the power to remove the principle of life from others (3 Macc. 6:24) and to give up his own (4 Macc. 12:19) but he cannot call it back again. (Wis. 16:14). The πνεῦμα of man may be withdrawn (Dan. 10:17 LXX) if only temporarily, and then be rekindled (Jud. 15:19, I Macc. 13:17) but this may be only a reference to physical breath. If this does refer to the πνεῦμα as the principle of life it has interesting ramifications not only for the theology of resurrection but for some of the present day ethical questions in medicine related to the use of life support systems.

In Ecclesiastes the word πνεῦμα appears to be used principally as a psychological expression whereas in Wisdom it signifies the very life-principle. In Wisdom this principle is considered to belong to God who loans it by breathing it into man. (15:11-16). In Wisdom also there is another πνεῦμα , which is identical with σοφία which does not come to man at the moment life begins but which may be imparted at a later time in answer to prayer. (7:7; 9:17).

The use of πνεῦμα in secular Greek may be categorized as follows:

I. WIND

In place of the Homeric πνοή the word πνεῦμα

occurs in both poetry and prose and denotes the wind, its invisibility and its movement as a blowing force. πνεῦμα is the most comprehensive word for "wind" and it readily and frequently assimilates the qualities of a variety of its synonyms, such as, πνοή , ἆημα , ἀήτη , ἄνεμος and ἀμδα . There is always a force in πνεῦμα and it is always associated with power. It is also associated with the idea of internal as well as external effects.

II. BREATH

Within the realm of organic life πνεῦμα is physiologically "the breath" which is inhaled or exhaled. This "breath" may include the strong "snorting" of an animal or the light and passing breath which fades like smoke and which represents the vanity of human life. The word is also used to denote the "voice" which is given to such inanimate objects as the flute by human "breath." This technical musical function of πνεῦμα gives point and relevance to Paul's comparison between spiritually effected "tongues" and the blowing of a flute or trumpet (I Cor. 14:7), for in tongues, as in blowing, a φωνή is called forth by πνεῦμα .[2]

III. LIFE

Breath is especially manifested by movement and thus is essentially a sign of life. Thus it comes to be that via the "breath of life" (πνεῦμα βίου) πνεῦμα comes to denote

---

[2]Kittel, Theological Dictionary of the New Testament, Vol. VI, p. 336.

a sense of life and eventually "living."

IV. SOUL

πνεῦμα   also takes on some of the significance
of "soul." These two terms while retaining certain and definite
distinctions eventually do overlap at certain points so that
both, for example, can be used to denote "the principle of
life."   πνεῦμα , however, is closely associated with the
physical aspects of man, while, at the same time, standing in
sharp contrast to the σῶμα with which it is bound in life.
At the moment of death it separates from the σῶμα for like
breath it escapes from the body with the last breath to return
to some upper region.

V. SYMBOLIC MEANING

In the metaphorical language of poetry the concrete
activity of breathing and blowing come to represent certain
psychological and spiritual processes. Thus πνεῦμα comes
to denote the unseen but experienced breath or spirit which
blows in relationships between people horizontally or between
the Divine and the human vertically. Thus when πίστις   dies
and ἀπιστια reigns the effect is that another "wind blows in
the affairs of men or of the state," and "the same spirit is
not present" as it was formerly between citizens and states.[3]
Thus, in accordance with its etymology πνεῦμα   is often used
to denote abstract concepts especially those of affective hyperthymia or excitement. This use is of importance for New Testament

---

[3]Kittel, Theological Dictionary of the New Testament,
Vol. VI, p. 336.

studies in that under such affective hyperthymia a man may loose control of his tongue (γλῶσης ἀκρατής   ), or he may utter confused words (θολεροὶ λόγοι   ) of a type of glossolalia.

VI.   **πνεῦμα and νοῦς**

Though closely related it is clear that two essentially different forms of the being and activity of the spirit are expressed by νοῦς and πνεῦμα   . πνεῦμα   always retains the basic idea of a powerful and moving breath, with all its associated functions, in both man and the world. In contrast with νοῦς the basic idea of πνεῦμα   remains that of something basically dynamic and vital. νοῦς   is to πνεῦμα   as light, with its accuracy and yet neutrality, is to wind which permeates and fills up and which is affect producing.

VII.   **μαντικον πνεῦμα**

πνεῦμα   also came to acquire a mantic flavor and especially in poetic language, came to signify the breath which inspires and fills. It also was applied to the convincing and persuasive rhetoric of literary asthetics where it meant "not so much the inspiration, but rather the expressive and captivating flow of the orator or poet from whom the onrushing "breath" of poetry or address comes forth neither physically, spiritually, nor technically."[4]

VIII.   **θεῖον πνεῦμα**

Because it was viewed as something non-corporeal,

---

[4]Kittel, <u>Theological Dictionary of the New Testament</u>, Vol. VI, p. 338.

uncontrollable and yet powerful πνεῦμα in the Greek mind
soon came to be viewed as something divine. However, it must
be noted that as yet there is no concept of πνεῦμα ἅγιον in
secular Greek. "Here biblical Greek has coined a new and destructive expression for the very different, suprasensual, supra-
terrestrial and in part personal character and content which
πνεῦμα has in Judaism and Christianity."[5] The uniqueness of
the term was also accepted in Latin where it was translated by
the original expression "spiritus sanctus."

IX. <u>σεος πνεῦμα</u>

As with many other basic concepts πνεῦμα , in its
development in profane Greek, reached its climax in the religious
philosophic concepts of Stoicism where it came to denote a
universal power and thus it came to be used linguistically for
the being and manifestation of deity itself.

<u>πνεῦμα in Greek Mythology and Religion</u>

The earliest concepts of πνεῦμα in Greek thought were
related to the relationships between man, his existence and
those of wind, breath and powers of generation. In the early
stages of development such ideas were expressed by the use of
synonyms such as ἐπίπνοια , ἐπιπνέω , ἄνεμος , ἀήρ
etc., and later these were all systematized under the single
term πνεῦμα . Wind, for example, was often thought of as
something which had life and being inherent within itself and

---

[5]Kittel, <u>Theological Dictionary of the New Testament</u>,
Vol. VI, p. 339.

which had no beginning. The wind, therefore, very easily came

to represent cosmologically a life-giving and generative force.

At times, therefore, the wind was considered to be a vehicle

of conception and to possess generative powers. It is not

surprising, therefore, to find that in one of the mythological

accounts of the creation of man, Zeus has the wind blow life

into his creatures and this idea is found very often in primitive

cosmologies. In the same way, a divine son was begotten by the

action of the breath of Zeus in both Egyption and Greek tradi-

tions.[6]

πνεῦμα   , to the Greek mind, was also the source of

inspiration. The πνεῦμα can impart a vital energy to man

which may even restore him to life. The Muses could create a

poet by breathing a divinely inspired voice into a man which

could result in prophetic powers but especially in an experience

of enthouiasm. This religious view of πνεῦμα and its associa-

tion with divine inspiration is found very early in Greek thinking,

first in the verb and later in the noun form of the word. It

came to represent the material force whose breath can result in

the estatic and rapturous in-filling by deity. It may produce

psycho-physiologic responses in the same way as the wind may

result in panting, etc. The filling with or by the πνεῦμα has

many effects which may range from fiery phenonema to the ability

to communicate oracles.

Of definite theological significance is the idea that

---

[6]Kittel, Theological Dictionary of the New Testament, Vol. VI, p. 341.

πνεῦμα   can be the cause of ecstatic speech in which a human agency is enabled to become "the divine voice." The activity of the πνεῦμα is seen characteristically to be related to like effects such as the sound of a rushing mighty wind of a stringed instrument. This, of course, is of much interest from the standpoint of New Testament studies where the same association is noted and where πνεῦμα is linked to προφητένειν   (Luke 1:67; 2 Pet. 1:21). Similarly it is noteworthy that πνεῦμα has a relationship to the spirit-given gift of tongues in Corinthians which may have been a reflection of Pythian prophesying there.

It is most interesting to note that Plato had definite views of the religious phenomenon of mantic ἐπίπνοια   . This could for example make a man "full of god," rob a man of understanding, enable him to prophesy and thus enable him to do much good even though he did not know what he was saying. He would not be speaking from himself or for himself but would, in fact, be used as a "ministering organ" by the god in question. This is the view of inspiration in secular Greek thinking and it is followed almost unquestioningly by Philo, Plutarch and even the early Christian Apologists.[7]

It is also worthy of note, that Plato considered it to be very important that the enthusiastic, ecstatic utterances of ϑεία ἐπίπνοια   be subject to examination and correct

---

[7]Kittel, Theological Dictionary of the New Testament, Vol. VI, p. 347.

appraisal. Reference here is made to the fact that the words of the Pythia often tended to torrent forth in a veritable ecstasy so that before they could be understood they required rearrangement, clarification and interpretation by the Delphic prophets or priests who possessed the gift of interpretation.

πνεῦμα in Hellenistic Judaism

I. Philo (Circa 20 B.C. - 54 A.D.)

In his psychology Philo considered that πνεῦμα played a role in the question of the essence of the soul. He described both blood and πνεῦμα as the soul's essence. The beasts had a non-rational soul which had its essence in blood, while man had a rational soul which is related to πνεῦμα. Man as a rational being is πνεῦμα but he is also the recipient of a divine πνεῦμα which is breathed into Him.

II. Josephus (Circa 37 - 100 A.D.)

The usage of Josephus is closely related to that of the LXX and of Philo. ψυχή as well as πνεῦμα is considered to be contained in αἷμα.

Summary

1. πνεῦμα originally meant the wind and nothing more and the origin of the word was undoubtedly based on onomatopoiea.

2. The earliest Greek word for wind was πνοή but from the time of Herodtus πνεῦμα was used for this purpose.

3. πνεῦμα next came to mean breath and then the principle of life.

4. God sends this vital principle and withdraws it at the moment of death.

5. πνεῦμα is always associated with force and with the effects produced by this force.

6. πνεῦμα is, on occasion, used to denote the voice.

7. At certain points πνεῦμα and ψυχή overlap so that, for example, both can be used to denote the life principle.

8. πνεῦμα is often used to denote a variety of psychological processes.

9. Though πνεῦμα is closely related to νοῦς it is clear that two essentially different forms of the being and activity of the spirit are expressed.

10. Especially in poetic literature and language πνεῦμα came to possess a mantic and inspirational aspect.

11. Since it was considered to be something powerful, non-corporeal and uncontrollable πνεῦμα soon came to be viewed as being divine in nature although, there was no concept of πνεῦμα ἅγιον in secular Greek.

12. In the religious philosophic concepts of Stoicism πνεῦμα came to denote a universal power and came to be used linguistically for the being and manifestation of deity itself.

13. For Philo πνεῦμα was related to the essence of the soul and was possessed by man as a rational being.

Chapter XIV

πνεῦμα IN THE NEW TESTAMENT, THE PAPYRI AND
THE APOSTOLIC FATHERS

As is רוּחַ in the Old Testament so πνεῦμα in
the New Testament is used in a variety of ways:

I. <u>πνεῦμα Used of God the Father</u>

In John 4:24 we learn that "God in πνεῦμα ."
This refers to the Divine Nature of God the Father and is beyond
our ability to fully understand.

II. <u>πνεῦμα Used of God the Son</u>

When Christ was begotten in a body of flesh in
incarnation he became "a living soul." Following his resurrection
he became "a life-giving πνεῦμα ." "The first man Adam
became a living being (ψυχην ζωσάν); The last Adam, a life-
giving spirit" (πνεῦμα ζωοποιοῦν). (I Cor. 15:45).

With Christ the word is used to denote the divine aspect
of His nature in contrast to His humanness. Thus at the moment
of His resurrection He was made alive in or by His life-principle
of πνεῦμα . (1 Peter 3:18) "For Christ also hath once suffered for sins, the just for the unjust, that He might bring us
to God, being put to death in the flesh but made alive by the
<u>spirit</u>."

III. <u>πνεῦμα Used for God the Holy Spirit</u>

Because He is emphatically God the Holy πνεῦμα it

166

has often been erroneously concluded that the word πνεῦμα in
the New Testament almost always refers to Him. This notion is
almost ubiquitous and in fact is so widespread and unconsciously
accepted that it has even influenced the majority of translators
of the Bible. Thus, even where no definite article is found in
the Greek Text, because it is assumed that reference is made to
the Holy Spirit, an article is often supplied in the English
translation.

Similarly the translators have often felt free to add
capital letters to the word πνεῦμα where they have felt it
appropriate. The danger in this lies in the fact that the English
reader is given no indication that what he is reading is not
a translation but rather an interpretation. A most important
guide to when the word is used with reference to the person of
the Holy Spirit is the presence or absence of the definite
article. The context is also of great importance in this respect.
Both of these together will seldom leave any doubt as to when the
Person of the Holy Spirit is meant. For example:

    I.   Acts 5:3 - The πνεῦμα the Holy.

"But Peter said, Ananias, why hath Satan filled
thine heart to lie to the Holy Spirit, and to keep back part
of the price of the land?"

    II.   Acts 13:2 - The πνεῦμα the Holy Spirit said.

"As they ministered to the Lord, and fasted, the
Holy Spirit said, Separate me Barnabas and Saul for the work
unto which I have called them."

    III.   Acts 15:28 - It seemed good to the Holy πνεῦμα .

"For it seemed good to the Holy Spirit, and to us, to lay upon you no greater burden than these necessary things."

IV. Acts 28:25 - The πνεῦμα the Holy.

"And when they agreed not among themselves, they departed, after Paul had spoken one word, Well spoke the Holy Spirit by Isaiah, the prophet, unto our fathers,"

V. Matthew 28:19

"Go ye, therefore, and teach all nations, baptizing them in the name of the Father, and of the Son, and of the Holy Spirit."

VI. John 15:26

"But when the Comforter is come, whom I will send unto you from the Father, even the Spirit of truth, who proceedeth from the Father, he shall testify of me:"

The Holy Spirit was affiliated in a special manner with Christ and worked with Him during His earthly ministry. Speaking of this Girdlestone writes:

> The Lord Jesus, as man, possessed spirit, soul and body; and His spirit was in a special sense the dwelling place of the Holy Spirit. He was filled with the Spirit, which was given to Him without measure. He was guided in his movements by the Spirit; His wisdom and discernment, His power over evil demons, and perhaps we may say all His words and deeds were wrought through the agency of the Spirit.[1]

There is also some special operations of the Holy Spirit which are the result of the completed work of Christ. On the foundation of the death, burial and resurrection of Jesus the

---

[1]R. B. Girdlestone, Synonyms of the Old Testament, p. 61-62.

Holy Spirit was poured out at Pentecost (Acts 2:4); an impetus to missionary activity was given and the mystery of the church as the body of Christ was unfolded (Ephesians 3:9 & 16).

VII. πνεῦμα Used as a Pronoun

πνεῦμα , like ψυχή in the New Testament, is often used pronominally and reflexively to indicate the "self" or the "whole person," as the part represents the whole. In such cases "my πνεῦμα " means "myself" even as ψυχή is used reflexively in Luke 1:47, where "my ψυχή " means "myself." Similarly in Mark 2:8 we learn that Jesus "perceived in His πνεῦμα " which simply means that Jesus perceived within Himself or that He had awareness within the totality of His own psychological processes. This corresponds exactly to Mark 5:30 where we learn that Jesus knew "in Himself."

VIII. πνεῦμα Used Adverbially

Numerous examples of πνεῦμα used in adverbial sense occur in the New Testament. The word may be used either with a simple dative or with a preposition. Examples are as follows:

a) ἐν τάχει SPEEDILY REV 1:1
b) ἐν δυνάμει POWERFULLY ROM 1:4
c) ἐν τῷ κρυπτῷ INWARDLY ROM 2:29
ἐν κρυπτῷ SECRETLY JOHN 18:20
d) ἐν ἀφροσύνῃ FOOLISHLY 2 COR 11:17

Thus the phrase ἐν πνεύματι may sometimes mean "spiritually," or "in a spiritual manner," and may not necessarily imply instrumental agency as is the case in Rev. 1:10 where the emphasis is on the agency of the Holy Spirit. It is to be noted, however, that both senses do over-lap because if something is accomplished by the agency of the Holy Spirit it will most certainly be done in a spiritual manner. This use of the word, therefore, comes to denote spiritually in the sense of essentially and intrinsically, and implies that whatever is done is carried out is in the highest degree, in the strongest form or in the highest measure. Thus, in this usage, the word πνεῦμα comes to indicate a superlative quality. For example the phrase "fervent in πνεῦμα " refers to what is exceedingly fervent rather than to any specific psychological functions.

The clear distinction between these two uses of the word may be seen in an examination of Acts 21:4 and 19:21. In the former the Holy Spirit clearly says that Paul "should not go up to Jerusalem." In the later, however, we learn that "Paul proposed in his πνεῦμα " to do this very thing. Since the Holy Spirit obviously cannot contradict himself or give to Paul two mutually contradictory messages, the use of πνεῦμα in the former verse must be different than its use in the latter. When Acts 19:21 indicates that Paul proposed in his πνεῦμα it simply means that Paul made his decision with strength and determination using the totality of his psychological processes.

IX. <u>πνεῦμα Used to Indicate the Operations of the</u>
<u>Holy Spirit</u>

In John 3:6 we read that "that which is born of the πνεῦμα is πνεῦμα ." In this verse there are two separate and distinct uses of the word πνεῦμα . Firstly, it is used to denote God the Holy Spirit, the second person of the Trinity. Secondly, there is that which is born out of (ἐκ) or produced as a result of His activity, namely, His operations and gifts which are also called πνεῦμα . In I COR 12(7-11) we have described for us what these spiritual operations and gifts are, namely:

1) Word of wisdom

2) Word of knowledge

3) Faith

4) Healing

5) Miracles

6) Prophecy

7) Discerning of Spirits

8) Tongues

9) Interpretation of tongues

X. πνεῦμα Used for the New Nature

In a very special sense the word πνεῦμα is used to indicate the new nature which is the greatest of all His spiritual gifts. This is particularly a Pauline usage. This new nature is the direct result of the activity of the Holy Spirit and is, therefore, according to John 3:6 "spirit" or πνεῦμα . All who possess this new nature are said to be "begotten of God." This new nature or πνεῦμα , not the believer, in the believer is "perfect" and "doth not commit sin" (I John 3:9 and 18). The old nature, which in contrast to the new is called "flesh," cannot but sin (Rom. 8:7). It is described as being at enmity with God and it is not subject to the Law of God, nor indeed, can it be.

A number of special uses of πνεῦμα occur when it is used to describe the new nature. It is called, for example, the πνεῦμα θεοῦ ; i.e., God's πνεῦμα or Divine Spirit since we are made "partakers of the Divine Nature." (2 Pet. 1:4) It is called the πνεῦμα of God because it comes from God. Similarly, it is called the πνεῦμα χριστοῦ or Christ's πνεῦμα because it is in virtue of this new nature that we are considered as being made the "sons of God" (Rom. 8:14). As possessors of the πνεῦμα of Christ, we are looked on as being children of God, heirs and joint-heirs with Christ (Rom. 8:17). Hence it is spoken of as "Son-Ship πνεῦμα ."

This use of πνεῦμα to denote the new nature and the new vital principle of the regenerate man is a characteristically Pauline usage. This πνεῦμα is very different from natural πνεῦμα which results in physical life. This new πνεῦμα is the result of inbreathing by the Holy Spirit and results in spiritual life which enables man to have communion with God and to cry "Abba Father." It is this inbreathing and its consequent life which is contrasted with natural life and its effects in John 3:6.

"That which is born of the flesh is flesh (natural flesh produces natural flesh which is energized by natural πνεῦμα), but that which is born of the Spirit is spirit" and possesses a new life energizing principle.

The use of πνεῦμα to refer to this new life principle

in the regenerate man is very much Pauline. Gould expresses

this aspect of the teaching of Paul very clearly:

> We must not think of the human spirit as the
> essential factor in the new man according to Paul.
> The essential factor is the Divine Spirit, who effects
> deliverance for the man not by creating or awakening
> a new faculty in him, but by coming Himself to dwell
> in him. This is the reason why it is the Holy Spirit,
> not the human spirit, that is constantly brought into
> contrast with the "flesh" in Paul......The human spirit
> is evidently the part in which, and upon which, the
> Holy Spirit works, and through which it controls the
> man, but which has no office except in connection with
> the Divine Spirit. Without the Divine Spirit it is
> like ears in a soundless world. The real agent in
> substituting holiness instead of sin in man is God,
> not man.[2]

Thus Paul in his writings considers the whole man to

be transformed as a result of the regenerating power of the

Spirit. The human Ego, energized only by natural $\pi\nu\epsilon\tilde{\upsilon}\mu\alpha$ -energy

recognizes the law of God but is unable to keep it. (Rom 7:14,

25). However the inbreathing of the new $\pi\nu\epsilon\tilde{\upsilon}\mu\alpha$ life principle

is ego-syntonic in nature so that the born again man is then

made "free from the law of sin and death" as a result of "the

law of the Spirit $\pi\nu\epsilon\tilde{\upsilon}\mu\alpha$ of life in Christ Jesus (Rom. 8:2).

In this power man is enabled to rise about the flesh, the

unregenerate nature, and live in the spirit (Rom 8:9). The new

$\pi\nu\epsilon\tilde{\upsilon}\mu\alpha$ is then working synergistically with the natural

$\pi\nu\epsilon\tilde{\upsilon}\mu\alpha$ to control behavior and to maintain communion with God."

The Spirit himself beareth witness with our spirit, that we are

children of God. (Rom. 8:16) This synergic activity will result

in God honoring behaviors and attitudinal styles such as:

---

[2]E. P. Gould, Article in the Biblical Encyclopaedia.

a)   a spirit of meekness   1 Cor. 4:21

b)   a spirit of wisdom   Eph. 1:17

c)   a spirit of holiness   Rom. 1:4

Cremer[3] summarizes this aspect of πνεῦμα   as follows:

"After all has been said, we must in general claim for πνεῦμα

two distinct meanings: spirit as the life-principle, or the

life-determining power, and spirit as a form of manifestation."

Speaking to the same issue Laidlaw writes:

> There are two things mainly noticeable and distinctive
> in this biblical use of "spirit." The first is the habit
> of biblical writers to explain the "spirit" in the
> natural man as the product or creation directly of God,
> and as accounted for only by the direct contact of man
> with the Almighty in his origin. This is peculiarly
> prevalent in the Old Testament (Genesis 2:7, Isaiah 42:5).
> Then there is the assertion of a parallelism and communi-
> cation between the self-conscious, inner life of man--his
> spirit--with the Spirit of God (I Corinthians 2:11, 12;
> Romans 8:1-17, Philemon 25). There is a foundation laid
> in this way for the whole spiritual life of man, and
> especially for the renewed and redeemed life of which,
> according to Christianity, he is made a partaker.[4]

XI.   πνεῦμα   Used Psychologically

The word πνεῦμα   is also used to describe man's

nature from the psychological point of view as He has been

created according to Genesis 2:7. For this reason in James 4:5

it is used to describe the totality of the old nature. By the

union of the "body" and the " πνεῦμα   " man becomes "a living

soul" or living being. When the body returns to the dust "as

it was" (Gen. 3:19) the πνεῦμα   returns to the God who gave

it. (Ecc. 12:7; Psalm 104:29-30). Hence at death the πνεῦμα

[3]Hermann Cremer, Biblico-Theological Lexicon of New
Testament Greek, Translated from the German of the second edition.
Edinburgh: T & T Clark, 1878.

[4]J. B. Laidlaw, Article on "Spirit" in Hastings Bible
Dictionary, p. 612.

is "commended" to God for His keeping (Psa. 31:5;
Luke 23:46; Acts 7:59) until it shall be reunited with the body
in resurrection.

It is noteworthy that while man possesses πνεῦμα   he
is never called a πνεῦμα   , as angels are. They are spiritual
beings whereas man is a human being. All persons, saved and
unsaved, have πνεῦμα   psychologically but not all have the
Divine nature.

In this connection it is useful to consider πνεῦμα as
the integrating life energy which separates the animate from
the inanimate. In the case of man this energy comes directly
from God and is sometime more than Freud's postulated psychoanalytic life force or the energy associated with cerebral neurophysiologic processes. It is this energy which when "breathed"
into a cadaverous σῶμα   causes it to become a living ψυχή
or functioning human personality or being. When such an individual is later regenerated an addition is made to his personality,
namely, the πνεῦμα   of God which causes him to be πνευματικός
and controlled by the Holy Spirit. It is the presence of the
energizing force of the Holy Spirit within the human personality
which constitutes the essential psychological difference between
the saved and the unsaved person. As will be noted later it is
suggested that it is not the person of Holy Spirit, but His power
which resides within the personality.

πνεῦμα   is used to represent the life principle which
is breathed into man by God and which gives him life. This use
is seen in Matthew 27:50 where Jesus "cried again with a loud

voice and yielded up his spirit (πνεῦμα). It is also used
to denote the return of the active principle of life in the case
of the daughter of Jairus, (Luke 8:55) "And her spirit came
again, and she arose straightway; and he commanded to give her
food." A similar use is seen in the case of Stephen (Acts 7:59);
"And they stoned Stephen, calling upon God, and saying, Lord
Jesus, receive my spirit." A more detailed use and explanation
of this use of the word is given by Jesus in John 6:63, "It is
the spirit that giveth life; the flesh profiteth nothing. The
words that I speak unto you, they are spirit, and they are life."
It is the πνεῦμα from God which gives physical life to the
flesh. In an analogous manner the very words of Jesus in regeneration result in new life in the personality.

XII. πνεῦμα Used of Personality Traits

Personality traits may be defined in psychological
terms as acquired or learned patterns of reactions. The word
πνεῦμα is used to denote such traits in a number of instances.

In 2 Tim. 1:7 we read of "a πνεῦμα of cowardice"
or a cowardly spirit. Similarly 1 Cor. 4:21 speaks of "a πνεῦμα
of meekness" or a meek spirit. Jesus speaks of those who were
"poor in their πνεῦμα " or of those whose outstanding personality characteristics were humility and meekness (Matt. 5:3).
Similarly, Paul in Rom. 8:15 speaks of a πνεῦμα of bondage,
namely, a bond-servant spirit and of a πνεῦμα of sonship or
of a sonship πνεῦμα.

XIII. πνεῦμα Used for Cognition and Affect

πνεῦμα is also used psychologically to denote the
cognitive and affective processes of the human mind. The word

is apparently chosen in this connection because such mental
processes are invisible and non-corporeal in contrast to "the
flesh." This contrast is clearly seen in Matt. 26:41 where
"the πνεῦμα is willing but the flesh is weak." In neurophysiologic and neuropsychologic language the limbic system of
the brain proved to be stronger than mere cognitive processes
and so the individual, like Paul in Romans Chapter 7, was in
a state of cognitive - emotive dissonance.

This is the use of the word in John 11:33 where the
emphasis is on the affect component of the experience of Jesus.

πνεῦμα is also used in connection with:

a.   The affect of anger.

Acts 17:16

"Now while Paul waited for them at Athens, his
spirit was stirred in him, when he saw the city wholly given
to idolatry."

b.   The affect of joy.

Luke 1:46

"And Mary said, My soul doth magnify the Lord,"

c.   The affect of enthusiasm.

Acts 18:25

"This man was instructed in the way of the Lord;
and, being fervent in the spirit, he spoke and taught diligently
the things of the Lord, knowing only the baptism of John."

XIV.   πνεῦμα Used of Evil Spirit-Beings

In I Tim. 4:1 we learn the "the Holy Spirit speaketh
expressly, that, in the latter times, some shall depart from the

faith, giving heed to deceiving πνεύματα , and teachings of demons." This could imply that there is a distinction between evil spirit beings or angels and demons. However, it would appear more likely that Paul is describing the evil πνεύματα and also the deceptive and erroneous teachings which come from this source.

πνεῦμα is thus used to denote evil spirit beings which are non-corporeal and immaterial. These spirit beings have the ability to demonize men and produce a variety of physical and psychiatric disturbances. It therefore appears most often with the modifier ἀκάθαρτον as, for example, in Matthew 10:1:

"And when he had called unto him his twelve disciples, he gave them power against <u>unclean spirits</u>, to cast them out, and to heal all manner of sickness and all manner of disease."

The effect of this evil being is noted in the production of a physical symptom in Mark 9:17:

"And one of the multitude answered and said, Master, I have brought unto thee my son, who hath a <u>dumb spirit</u>;"

XV. πνεῦμα <u>Used of Good Spirit-Beings</u>

πνεῦμα is also used to indicate good spirit beings which are non-corporeal and immaterial, i.e., angels. It is rarely used in this manner in the New Testament. Examples of this usage are:

a. <u>Hebrews 1:14</u>

"Are they not all ministering spirits, sent forth to minister for them who shall be heirs of salvation?"

b. <u>Revelation 1:4</u>

"John, to the seven churches which are in Asia:
Grace to unto you, and peace, from him who is, and who was,
and who is to come, and from the seven spirits who are before
his throne;"

πνεῦμα is also used to describe good angels or
spirit-beings which are distinct from human-beings or "flesh
and blood" (I Cor. 15:50). They are also distinct from the
human body in resurrection which has "flesh and bones" (Luke
24:39) and is therefore not a true angel or spirit-being.

XVI.   πνεῦμα   Used of the Resurrection Body

As we have just noted πνεῦμα is used of the
resurrection body which is distinct from an angelic body and
also from a purely human body. Angels have never had a human
body but in resurrection the christian will have had a human
body and so in resurrection he can be made like his risen glori-
ous Lord. (Phil. 3:21). The resurrection body will be a
πνεῦμα -body or spirit-body distinct from both angels and
humans and yet possessing "flesh and bones."

XVII.   πνεῦμα   Used of "Wind," or Air in Motion

There are only a few references in which the word
is used to denote wind as air in motion and nothing more. Such
a usage is seen in John 3:8: "The wind bloweth where it willeth,
and thou hearest the sound of it, but canst not tell from where
it cometh, and where it goeth; so is every one that is born of
the Spirit."

The word may also be used with this same connotation
in Hebrews 1:7, "And of the angels he saith, Who maketh his
angels spirits, and his ministers a flame of fire." The reference

to the angels as πνεύματα may be an allusion to the wind-like character of angels rather than the fact that God created them as spirit beings.

πνεῦμα in the Papyri

The word πνεῦμα is found quite commonly in the Papyri and possesses a variety of meanings.

a. In a fragment from the Oxyrhynchus Papyri it signifies "breath."

"who am daily suspended by ropes and have my body belabored with blows, and possess no brother, no relative, no son to sympathize with me, so that at last the very breath (πνεῦμα) of my life is in danger."[5]

b. In another Oxyrhynchus Papyri it is translated "winds"

"Shut off the winds (πνεύματα), and night, grant the waters to be smooth."[6]

c. The influence of secular Greek, in contrast to Old Testament thinking, is seen in another fragment from the Oxyrhynchus Papyri, where the word appears to be used to give the notion of an intangible, non-corporeal "spirit."

"Here what it is necessary for you to do to save your spirit."[7]

It should, however, be noted that the word here may

---

[5] The Oxyrhynchus Papyri, Vol. 3, 6904.7.

[6] The Oxyrhynchus Papyri, Vol. 11, 1386.10.

[7] The Oxyrhynchus Papyri, Vol. 15, 1782.11.

be used simply as a synonym for the whole man which idea would then be perfectly consistent with Biblical Theology.

      d.   πνεῦμα   is also use to denote an evil spirit. Thus, a christian charm of the 5th Century A.D. was developed to ward off sicknesses and other evils. The first words of the charm were:

$$\text{"φεῦγε, πνεῦμα μεμισιμένον,}$$
$$\text{χρίστος σε διώκει προέλαβεν}$$
$$\text{ὁ υἱός θεοῦ καὶ τὸ}$$
$$\text{πνεῦμα τὸ ἅγιον."}$$

        "FLY, HATED SPIRIT (πνεῦμα   )!

        CHRIST PURSUE THEE - THE SON

        OF GOD AND THE HOLY SPIRIT HAVE

        OUT-STRIPPED THEE"[8]

      e.   The word is also used in the Papyri to denote members of the God-head.

      1.   The Father

        "They were destroyed because they departed from the living spirit (πνεῦματος   ) after their own lawlessness."[9]

        The contextual evidence here points to the reference being to God the Father.

      2.   Christ

        "He sent forth prophets to herald our Lord Jesus Christ, men who receiving in order and lot and due portion

---

    [8]The Oxyrhynchus Papyri, Vol. 8, 1151.1.6.

    [9]The Oxyrhynchus Papyri, Vol. 13, 1602.23.

of the Spirit of Christ"[10]

3. The Holy Spirit

"And many of them that believe on Him will speak through the Holy Spirit"[11]

f. The word is also used in the Papyri in at least a partially psychological sense of an attitude of power. Speaking of the last day, a reference from the Oxyrhynchus Papyri reads:

"And accept the word, because a spirit of power in the last time------"[12]

πνεῦμα in the Apostolic Fathers

The word πνεῦμα is used frequently in the Church Fathers and by this time in its development has acquired a variety of meanings. The following examples are from the Shepherd of Hermas.

1. πνεῦμα is used to denote the spirit or the vital principle of life within man, which was inbreathed into him by God.

"Why did she not appear to you in the first vision as old and seated in a chair? Because your spirit (πνεῦμα) is old and already fading away, and has no power through your weakness and double-mindedness----------but your mind was

---

[10]Ibid.

[11]The Oxyrhynchus Papyri, Vol. 15, 1792.11.

[12]The Oxyrhynchus Papyri, Vol. 13, 1602.39.

broken, and you grow old in your sorrows."[13]

2. πνεῦνα is also used in a wider sense to denote the whole man and not just a single aspect of his make-up.

"---which the Lord revealed to you, that he had mercy upon you, and renewed your spirit (πνεῦματα); and put aside your weakness."[14]

3. πνεῦμα is frequently used to indicate the Holy Spirit, the second person of the Trinity.

"---that the Spirit which God made to dwell in this flesh may be found true by all men----for they received from Him a Spirit free from lies."[15]

However, in this connection note the observations recorded elsewhere in this study as to whether it is the person of the Holy Spirit who comes to reside in a man or God's "power from on high."

4. It is used to denote an "evil spirit" in a context which makes it difficult to decide whether the author was using the term psychologically, demonologically or possibly with both senses.

"But if any ill temper enter, at once the Holy Spirit, which is delicate, is oppressed, finding the place unpure and seeks to depart out of the place, for it is choked by the evil spirit. (πονηροῦ πνεύματος)---for the Lord dwells

---

[13]Kirsopp Lake, The Apostolic Fathers, Vol. I, 3.11.2.

[14]Ibid.

[15]Kirsopp Lake, The Apostolic Fathers, Vol. I, Mand. 3.1.

in long-suffering and the devil dwells in ill Temper."[16]

The Spirit and Resurrection

In both Old and New Testaments spirit is intimately associated with resurrection. In the same manner that the entrance of רוּחַ or πνεῦμα into man at the moment of creation or conception gave him life, so at the moment of resurrection the restoration of the life-principle results in the renewal of life. An excellent illustration of this activity is seen in Ezekiel's vision of the valley of dry bones in Ezekiel, Chapter 37. Bones, which are described as being "very dry" and which once had life in them are seen to be with "no רוּחַ " in them (verse 8). Then comes the operation of the figurative wind, רוּחַ , breath or life-principle and life was restored as God caused רוּחַ to enter them again.

Ezekiel 37:5 - "Thus saith the Lord God unto these bones, Behold, I will cause breath to enter into you, and ye shall live."

Ezekiel 37:6 - "And I will lay sinews upon you, and will bring up flesh upon you, and cover you with skin, and put breath in you, and ye shall live; and ye shall know that I am the Lord."

Ezekiel 37:14 - "And shall put my Spirit in you, and ye shall live, and I shall place you in your own land; then shall ye know that I, the Lord, have spoken it, and performed it, saith the Lord."

Thus, as Froom notes,

---

[16]Kirsopp Lake, The Apostolic Fathers, Vol. I, Mand., 3.4.

The life that was relinquished when the spirit left
the body is thus renewed. And it was this renewal, or
restoration of the spirit, or breath-the breath of God
that caused life-that was the hope and the promise of
a future life for the Old Testament worthies. When
they knew they were dying, and were soon to sink back
into their original earth, they commended their spirits
into the safekeeping of God. Thus the Psalmist David,
upon the prospect of death, said: "Into thine hand I
commit my spirit (רוח): thou hast redeemed me,
O Lord God of Truth-----I trust in the Lord."
(Ps. 31:5,6).[17]

David was confident that his God, who had redeemed him,

and who at death had received his Spirit back again as a forfeit

for original sin, would restore him to life as He had promised.

Summary

1. πνεῦμα in the New Testament is the counterpart
of רוח in the Old Testament.

2. πνεῦμα is used to denote the persons of the
God-head.

3. πνεῦμα in the New Testament is used pronominally
and adverbially.

4. πνεῦμα is also used to denote the actual operations
of God the Holy Spirit.

5. πνεῦμα is used to denote the new nature of the
believer as well as the vital principle of regeneration.

6. πνεῦμα is also used psychologically to denote a
variety of psychological functions and personality traits.

7. πνεῦμα is used of both evil and good spirit

---

[17]L. F. Froom, The Conditionalist Faith of our Fathers,
p. 157.

beings but man is never called a πνεῦμα   as angels are.

8.   πνεῦμα   is used to indicate wind or air in motion.

9.   In the Papyri it is used as a synonym for the whole man as well as a variety of meanings already mentioned above.

10.   In the Shepherd of Hermas it is used to denote the life-principle as well as the whole man.

11.   In the same manner that the entrance of πνεῦμα gives life, and the entrance of the Holy Spirit gives new regenerate life so at the moment of resurrection the πνεῦμα revitalizes the body to result in resurrection life.

Chapter XV

CONCLUSION AND INTEGRATION

THE PSYCHOTHEOLOGY OF CONSCIENCE

In man there is an innate "law" written on the heart which acts as a moral barometer and which contains certain God given absolutes within the human personality. The psychic appartus also contains the conscience proper which corresponds to the συνείδησις of the New Testament. The development of this Superego has been discussed in detail and it has been noted that the origin of this organ lies in learned behavior and in particular in the introjection of a series of images with their associated values and standards. The function of the συνείδησις is to control the ego, or executive agent of the personality, by means of the "whip" of the Superego with the production of guilt-anxiety, or by means of the "carrot" of the Ego ideal with the production of shame-anxiety. The ego is constantly seeking not only to maintain psychic homeostasis but to do so at the expense of as little dysphoria as possible.

The "cardiac law" is the innate division of the psychic apparatus and it is perceived by the Superego or conscience proper by means of a vestigial consciousness which may well represent a remnant of the Imago Dei and which corresponds to "The light that lighteth every man that cometh into the world."

The conscience proper therefore looks in two directions: firstly, to the "cardiac law" and secondly, to the Ego as the executive of the personality. The Ego in this way is influenced in its executive decisions to either repress forbidden impulses or to express on the level of consciousness in an external behavior that which has received approbation.

The perceiving function of the conscience proper may be changed and blunted by sin so that it looses its ability to control the Ego and this conscious ideation and behavior. In the Christian the Ego ideal is reconstructed and is rendered much more acute in its functioning by the introjection of the image of Christ in the process of regeneration. In addition, the Ego is given additional strength by the permeating "power from on high" of the Holy Spirit and thus emulation of the behavior of Christ becomes a possibility.

THE PSYCHOTHEOLOGY OF SOUL

As we have seen, the concept of "soul" in both the Old and New Testaments is very different from what is considered to be the Orthodox view in the Christian church today. meant the intrinsic vitality and the various aspects of the psychological function of man. When a man showed movement he had life and this was נֶפֶשׁ . It was always connected with a form and was never considered to have any type of separate existence apart from the body. נֶפֶשׁ can best be translated as person or personality as it is the function of the total man which is in view when the word is used.

Similarly in the New Testament the concept of ψυχή is never that of an immortal metaphysical entity which has existence apart from the body. The word often refers to the Ego as the executive agent of the personality and is thus often used pronominally. It refers to the living quality of the total man and of his personality in function. It is not what a man has but what he is.

In all probability the first systematic formulation of the basic Greek and pagan presuppositions relative to the soul came with Augustine of Hippo. His view of the soul was completely Platonic. He viewed the soul as an immaterial indistructible non-physical metaphysical entity which could exist apart from the body and as something like the image on a Kirlian photograph. He emphasized the nature of man and even considered the soul to be a mirror of the divine nature, corresponding in its faculties to the Trinity itself. Augustine's writings profoundly influenced the development of Christian theological thinking down to and beyond Thomas Aquinas. The latter's view of the soul was slightly different from that of Augustine but he still was significantly influenced by neoplatonic ideas. It is not too surprising that the reformation theologians did not change the basic Platonic presuppositions in regard to the soul. They continued to develop their anthropology in the traditional manner of Christianized pagan Greek ideas. Calvin for example thus speaks of soul as "an immortal, yet created essence----and incorporeal substance."[1] As previ-

---

[1] John Calvin, Institutes of the Christian Religion, Vol. 1, No. 15, Grand Rapids, Erdmans, 1957.

ously noted, these ideas have continued to permeate Christian theologic thinking.

Luther's views on the nature of the soul are somewhat difficult to pin down. In A.D. the council of the Lateran made a pronouncement that the immortality of the soul, presumably as a separate and distinct entity, was to be numbered among the orthodox articles of the Christian Faith. It then added the following statement: "And we strictly inhibit from all dogmatizing otherwise; and we decree that all who adhere to the like erroneous assertions shall be shunned and punished as heretics." Martin Luther, however, soon demonstrated that on this point he was a "heretic" for in his Defence, Prop. 27, published in 1520, he said: "I permit the Pope to make articles of Faith for himself and for his faithful----such as the soul is the substantial form of the human body, that the soul is immortal, with all those monstrous opinions to be found in Roman dunghills of decretals." At that particular point in his career, it is therefore clear that Luther held a view significantly different from the orthodox position.

Berkhof, who may be considered as a representative of modern theological thinking, continued to accept the basic Platonic presuppositions regarding the soul. He developed a theory of "realistic dualism" to explain the relationship between the body and soul and said "the body and soul are distinct substances, which do interact, though their mode of interaction escapes human scrutiny and remains a mystery to us----from the continued conscious existence and activity of the soul after death it appears that it can also work without the body."[2]

Similarly, Chafer, who may be considered a representative of the Evangelical school, followed the classical line
of thinking although he demonstrates some significant insights.
Speaking of the distinction between the material and immaterial
part of man or between soul and body he stresses that at death
they are separated, the one from the other. "Though material
and immaterial parts of man are often set over against each
other and reference is made to them as component parts of man's
being, man is, nevertheless, a unity--one being--and the material
and immaterial can be separated only by physical death. There
is a psychology which treats man as an integer, a monad, and
asserts that the immaterial part of man is not the man, nor is
the material part the man; but that he is the tertium quid of
both elements united. Naturally, there is a ground on which
this thesis might rest, but the Bible definitely and constantly
separates these two factors in man's being. The logical conclusion of this psychology is that death is the end of man's
existence since the body so obviously ceases to function and
decays, and that man's immaterial part, being, as supposed,
inseparable from the body, must suffer the same fate. Over
against this, the Scriptures teach with clearness that man,
though a unity, is composed of separable parts. While the immaterial part of man resides in the body, the sense of unity is
all that man experiences. At death these elements are separated

---

[2]L. Berkhof, _Systematic Theology_, pp. 191 ff., Grand
Rapids, 1941.

for a season, only to be reunited in God's appointed time and way. It is thus demonstrated that those two parts are separable."[3]

In spite of heavy assertions such as these, it is the conviction of this author that the traditional view of the soul derived as it has been from pagan, Hellinistic speculative thinking is not synonomous with the Biblical concept and that the concept of "soul" as something within and separate from man is meaningless. All Christians will agree that the Bible as the inspired word of God is the final answer and the foundation for our Christian beliefs. It therefore is imperative that we constantly examine the traditional against the revealed. This is particularly difficult for us to do when we attempt to examine such a "sacred cow" as the traditional concept of the soul. It is, however, imperative that we make this examination because it is frequently such traditional thinking which makes us suspect by our colleagues in the behavioral sciences and causes them to voice strong criticisms of religious thinking in general since it indulges itself in metaphysical speculations which bear no relationship to observed phoenomena.

It is the conviction of this author that the Biblical idea of soul is consistent with the views of modern psychology and that it is this concept alone which stresses the wholeness of man. As Howard has very adequately pointed out, there is nothing by which we can qualitatively distinguish man from other animals. He says "while there may be differences in degree,

_____

[3]L. S. Chafer, Systematic Theology, pp. 146-147, Dallas Seminary Press, 1964.

there is no absolute difference in biological terms between
man, and say the higher apes. On the other hand the Judeao-
Christian tradition affirms that man stands as distinct from
the rest of the animal creation."[4] He emphasizes, as does the
Biblical record, that man was created in the "image of God"
but he denies the traditional viewpoint which would imply that
this means that man has some kind of spiritual and additional
aura or "form" namely the soul. He points out some of the
unique characteristics of man, for example, that man alone is
capable of making value judgements, man alone is the only creature
that the Biblical record presents as being able to cooperate
as a willing agent in the purposes of God and it was only through
a Man that God chose to redeem His creation.

In attempting any integration of theological and psychological thinking on the subject of the soul it is well to remember that much loose thinking has occurred in both fields. As
we have seen the use of the word $\psi\upsilon\chi\acute{\eta}$ in Scripture does not
support the common theological interpretation of the soul as
a non-physical and separate metaphysical appendage to man.
Similarly the thinking found in many of the schools of psychology is characterized by speculation unsupported by scientifi-
cally based observation. Since the Bible is truth, we can be
assured that when psychology finds truth, then psychology and
theology will be in complete harmony.

Man must be considered as a totality "in function," as

---

[4]J. K. Howard, The Concept of the Soul in Psychology
and Religion, Journal of the American Scientific Affiliation,
Vol. 24, No. 4, December, 1972.

an organism which expresses the vitality of his existence
through his functioning. This is his personality. It is the
observed and observable phenomena of the total life manifested
primarily through interpersonal relationships.[5] Personality
can only be understood in terms of community---the community
of man to man and man to God. This is included in the idea
of wholeness which is basic to both a psychological and theological anthropology. Mans redemption is never considered apart
from his corporeal nature and must include the total man and
no part of man has any existence in its own right in isolation.
The soul cannot be equated with Id, Ego, or Superego but with
the total "person"; the whole human organism. As Nelson has
so succently stated "personality is the person in the situation"[6]
or as has already been stated the total man "in function." When
this concept of personality is considered as an interlocking
of functions and traits, an architectural unity involving the
whole person, it will be seen to closely equate the Biblical
use of $\psi\upsilon\chi\acute{\eta}$ and no disharmony will be seen to exist between
theological and psychological thinking.

THE PSYCHOTHEOLOGY OF SPIRIT

Let it again be emphasized that the use of any model
of human personality is only as good as its effectiveness in
explaining the phenomenology of man. The great danger lies in

---

[5]W. L. Carrington, Psychology, Religion and Human Need,
London, 1957, p. 40.

[6]H. Nelson, Adaption-Level Theory; An Experimental and
Systematic Approach to Behavior, New York, 1964, p. 541.

the fact that sometimes the model may be viewed as objective reality rather than a mere, but very useful, tool for describing and understanding that reality. When this is understood, the notion of spirit as energy is most useful as phenomenology is approached analogically. As we cannot isolate the Ego or Superego so similarly we cannot isolate, much less measure "Psychic energy" and even less can we expect to put any physical measurement on the "power from on high."

It has been seen that both in Hebrew and Greek thought the spirit is the life principle which comes from God and which returns to him at the moment of death. It is thus impersonal and is merely the life force which differentiates the animate from the inanimate. It is the interaction of this life force with the body of clay which eventuates in ψυχή, or the living personality. It is this energetic life principle which gushes up from the deep layers of the personality and which is mediated into a variety of psychological processes, ideation and behavior. The quality and quantity of a man's behavior is the result of his capacity to filter, modify and use this basic energy source and its derivatives.

In the same way the "power from on high" which is re- ceived at and is a vital part of the regeneration process, may be thought of as a supply of power and energy. This is in effect an addition to the personality and forms an additional reservoir of energy which may be used for a variety of psychological processes and in particular for the control of behavior so that a Christ-like image is emulated. This spirit is, in addition,

the life-principle of the personality which makes the individual
a new creature now alive spiritually to God.

THE PSYCHOTHEOLOGY OF THE CONSTITUTION
OF MAN: DICHOTOMOUS OR TRICHOTOMOUS

The question of the number of the constituent elements
in the human constitution has long been a matter of consideration
and discussion in Christian Theology. The trichotomist insists
that man is a tripartite being who is composed of body, soul,
and spirit. The dichotomist, on the other hand, considers man
to be bipartite in nature, being composed of a material body and
an immaterial soul and/or spirit. This question is an interesting
one from the scientific and psychological point of view and it
also is of theological importance.

It may also be noted that as the Old Testament anthropology
is concerned, Israelite anthropology was strongly monistic. Man
was always seen in His totality. The unity of human nature was
not expressed by the concepts of body and soul but by the comple-
mentary and inseparable concepts of body and life.[7]

The scriptures, as the inspired Word of God, do not claim
to be a textbook of science of psychology. However, if they are
indeed the inspired Word of God _in toto_, then the material contained in them will be found to be psychologically correct when
the facts of science are finally validated as truth. It is also
true that God used the idioms and the modes of expression current
in the various cultures in which the word of God was given. Yet

---

[7]Kittel, Vol. IX, p. 631.

since God is the author of truth and all truth is one, the
content of Scripture will always agree with science finally
validated.

The whole difficulty regarding the number of constituent
elements in the makeup of man lies in the fact that some passages
appear to speak trichotomously while others speak dichotomously.
For example, in the following passages what appears to be a
trichotomist form will be found: 1 Thessalonians 5:23, "And
the very God of peace sanctify you wholly; and I pray God your
whole spirit and soul and body be preserved blameless unto the
coming of our Lord Jesus Christ." The same idea is contained
in Hebrews 4:12, "For the word of God is living, and powerful,
and sharper than any two-edged sword, piercing even to the
dividing asunder of soul and spirit, and of the joints and
marrow, and is a discerner of the thoughts and intents of the
heart." In this latter verse a distinction appears to be made
between soul and spirit.

On the other hand, other verses appear to indicate a
dichotomous view. For example, in I Corinthians 6:20, the
apostle says, "For ye are bought with a price; therefore, glorify
God in your body and in your spirit, which are God's." A similar
view is seen in James 2:26, "For as the body without the spirit
is dead, so faith without works is dead also." This immediately
raises the question, "Is man composed of two essences, the
material forming the body and a spiritual essence also called
'soul' which as the life principle organizes the bodily structure;
or is there besides the matter of the body and the rational

πνεῦμα   also ψυχή or a 'soul' as the life principle of
the bodily organism and the source of the lower passions and
instincts?"[8]

The following is a summary of some of the facts used
in support of the tripartite view.

I.   There is a tripartite view implied in many languages.

1.   Hebrew

בָּשָׂר

נֶפֶשׁ

רוּחַ and its synonym   נְשָׁמָה

2.   Greek
εῶμα
ψυχή
πνεῦμα

3.   Latin

Corpus

Anima

Animus or Mens

4.   German

Leib

Seele

Geist

5.   English

Body

Soul

Spirit

6. French

Corps

Ame

Espirit

II.   A tripartite view may be noted in some of the very early attempts at a philosophic view of man.

1.   PLATO

Plato held to a three-fold division of man as follows:

a.   Soul as desire or affection

(τὸ ἐπιθυμητικόν   )

b.   Passion or courage (τὸ θυμοειδές   )

c.   Reason (τὸ λογιστικόν   ). For Plato reason was immortal.

2.   ARISTOTLE

Aristotle considered man to be composed of

a.   σῶμα

b.   ψυχή

c.   νοῦς   The νοῦς for Aristotle was the principle of rational intelligence which existed before the body and which entered it as something divine and immortal. He also considered that with men animals possessed σῶμα   and ψυχή but that man alone possessed the rational principle (νοῦς) as his unique endowment.

3.   PLOTINUS

Plotinus was the great neo-platonist and he developed the concept of a full trichotomy.

a. The reason (νοῦς) comes to man directly from the Creator.

b. This produces a soul (ψυχή) as its image.

c. Both νοῦς and ψυχή precede and survive the σῶμα (body).

It was probably from this neo-Platonic orientation that Apollinaris was to later develop the idea that Christ did not possess a rational soul and that the Divine Logos took its place.

During the early years of the church the view of man was generally trichotomistic especially among writers of the Alexandrian School. Justin Martyr, Irenaeus, Origen, Clement of Alexandria taught a tripartite view as did the Gnostics. As time went on, however, trichotomy declined and was superseded by the simpler and more Biblical view of dichotomy. In the fourteenth century however Occam favored the trichotomous view. He distinquished between the thinking mind (anima intellectiva) and the feeling soul (anima sensitiva). He also taught that the intellective soul was a different substance than the sensitive soul and that it was capable of a separate existence apart from the body.[9]

Delitzsch's view was that man had been created as a physical and unvitalized organism. God then imparted the spirit-energy or the breath of life which was the origin of man's human spirit. This spirit-energy then vitalized the body which

---

[9]Milton Valentine, Christian Theology, Vol. I, pp. 385-393, The United Lutheran Publication House, Philadelphia, PA, 1906.

produced the animal soul. "The soul is related to the spirit as life to the principle of life, and as effect to that which produces it." This view which Delitzsch considered to be "a True Trichotomy" is, in fact, a dichotomous view since the quickening spirit of God produces a human spirit and the "soul" becomes the effect of this implanted spirit.

The trichotomous view of man has failed to satisfy those psychologists who have cared to examine the problem. Vincent points this out in some detail.

> How thoroughly the Trichotomistic teaching has failed to hold the homage of recent psychology is seen in the fact that in Flemming's "Vocabulary of Philosophy," from thirty-seven different modern philosophers who have attempted to define the soul, only one presents a really Trichotomistic view, viz., Rothe. He says: "The spirit is something higher than the soul. In the spirit is the unity of our being, our true ego. The soul is but an element in its service. At death the soul passes away; the spirit reopens to a new existence.[10]

The evidence of scripture considered as a whole, appears to be against the trichotomous view. For example:

1. The Biblical statement as to the creation (Genesis 2:7) says the man was endowed by the inbreathing of the Spirit. No mention is made of man being endowed with a soul apart from the spirit.

2. James 2:26

"For as the body without the spirit is dead, so faith without works is dead also." This must mean that bodily life is dependent upon the life-principle of the spirit. Nothing

---

[10] Ibid., p. 460.

is said about a separate soul.

A few authors take a dichotomous view because they consider "soul" and "spirit" to be synonymous. The supporting data which they use may be summarized as follows:

1. The terms נֶפֶשׁ and ψυχή (soul) appear to be used as the equivalents of רוּחַ and πνεῦμα (spirit) in a number of passages.

2. "Glorify God in your body and in your spirit" sums up the whole man in two parts and appears to use πνεῦμα and ψυχή as equivalent terms.

In this connection is it useful to note the observations of Diogenes Laeritus in the third century. He commented on the relationship between ψυχή and πνεῦμα and indicated that Zenophon of Athens was the first to address ψυχή as πνεῦμα. The context in which this took place, however, appears as reference to the "perishable breath" which was often regarded as the essence of the soul. A study of the usage of the words would appear to support the conclusion that while at times the meanings overlap, e.g., in describing the psychological aspects of man, πνεῦμα and ψυχή have very clear differences.

If the dichotomous view is the correct one psychotheologically then what is the explanation for those texts which appear to favor the tripartite notion? The following observations are an attempt to do this and are based on the concepts of soul and spirit discussed in this work.

1. The term spirit refers to the completely impersonal energy of the personality of man. It separates the animate

from the inanimate and it is the spirit as the principle of life which returns to God, as the author of life, at the moment of death. The soul, on the other hand, represents the synthesis of spirit working with body to produce a living being or personality (soul).

2. There can, therefore, be no separate existence of a personal soul without a body. At the moment of death the body becomes inanimate as the πνεῦμα -spirit or life-principle returns to God. At that moment the body ceases to function and goes to sleep. The personality or "person in function" disappears and does not reappear until the πνεῦμα-energy returns to quicken the new body of "flesh and bone" at the moment of resurrection. As the new body, begins to function, personality will again appear.

3. When Paul prays that the "body soul and spirit" may be sanctified he is not presenting a psychological analysis of the constitution of man. He is merely praying that the whole man, "lock, stock and barrel," his body energized by his God given spirit to appear phenomenologically as a functioning personality or soul, may all be permeated by the grace of God and to stand thus before Christ in resurrection and at His coming.

THE PSYCHOTHEOLOGY OF THE IMAGO DEI

There are a number of specific declarations in the Scriptures that man has been created in God's image.

1. Genesis 1:26

"And God said, Let us make man in our image, after

our likeness; and let them have dominion over
the fish of the sea, and over the fowl of the air,
and over the cattle, and over all the earth, and
over every creeping thing that creepeth upon the
earth."

2. Genesis 1:27

"So God created man in his own image, in the image
of God created he him; male and female created he
them."

3. Genesis 5:1

"This is the book of the generations of Adam. In
the day that God created man, in the likeness of
God made he him;"

4. Genesis 9:6

"Whoso sheddeth man's blood, by man shall his blood
be shed; for in the image of God made he man."

The texts do not clearly state just in what way man can be said
to be in the image of God. This is a task for sound exegesis.

It has been stated, for example, that these verses teach
the unconditional immortality of man, i.e., the presence of a
disparate self-conscious soul, and since God has immortality
man must therefore be like Him in this respect. However, the
scriptures teach just the opposite in this particular case,
and they emphasize that God "only hath immortality" (I Timothy
6:15-16). In addition, it would be most unusual for the remain-
der of the entire Scripture record to be absolutely silent on
such an important subject, if that is indeed the impact of these

verses. There also appears to be no textual or contextual reason why this particular attribute of God should be singled out for support by these verses. If indeed innate immortality, based on a immortal soul, can be based on these texts then by the same reasoning so should such doctrines as the pre-existence of man or man's omniscience, omnipotence, omnipresence, etc.

It would appear to be more in agreement with the whole tenor of the Word to think of man's likeness to God has reference to a moral nature, which differentiates him from the animal creation. It would also seem reasonable that this likeness was to some degree marred in the Fall although vestigial remnants of it remain in the human personality as the "cardiac law" and the vestigial consciousness of this law.

THE PSYCHOTHEOLOGY OF REGENERATION AND THE DIFFERENCE BETWEEN THE SAVED AND THE UNSAVED INDIVIDUAL PSYCHOLOGICALLY

The natural man possesses all the constituent parts of the psychic apparatus which have already been examined in some detail. (Fig. 1) His natural endowment consists of the Id, which is the reservoir of his instinctual force, energy, or πνεῦμα . Within the psychoanalytic perspective, this basic instinctual energy is differentiated into the basic drives, namely, the sexual drive and the aggressive drive. In classic psychoanalytic theory and practice all behaviors are analyzable back to the expression of these two basic instinctual forces. These drives are never seen in pure culture but form the basic instinct fusion in which the aggressive instinct fusion has a lesser percentage of sexual drive and the sexual instinct fusion has a lesser percentage of the aggressive drive. At this level, the drives and their early derivatives are unconscious.

Early in life the differentiation of the Ego takes place. The first step of this differentiation is the recognition of the self versus non-self. The Ego develops initially in response to the differentiation of the self from non-self and becomes the executive agency of the personality, in that it mediates between conscious and unconscious processes. The Superego, with its attendant Ego ideal, is also differentiated as a sub-division of the Ego. It contains the repository of the values and also of the idealized image of the significant adult from the child's early years. The Ego is then called on to control the expression of the basic instinct fusions and their derivatives. The operation of this control is triggered by anxiety and in particular by the guilt-anxiety generated by the Superego and by the shame-anxiety of the Ego ideal. It is the Superego which is the συνείδησις of the New Testament and thus the συνείδησις contains both the Superego and the Ego ideal.

From Biblical revelation we learn, in addition, that every man contains a "cardiac law" which is "the light the lighteth every man that cometh into the world." This law is perceived by the Ego and especially by the Superego by means of remnants of the vestigial consciousness and is an innate representation of morality. All psychic processes, especially those of the Ego, require energy for successful operation.

This energy in the natural state comes from the reservoir of πνεῦμα -energy existing in the unconscious.

At the moment of regeneration, there is an augmentation of basic πνεῦμα -energy in the psychic apparatus by the incoming of "power from on high" which is a manifestation of the power of the Holy Spirit. With this increase in energy, the ego is then able to perform functions like repression and other defensive energy-requiring maneuvers and is able, there-fore, to perform them much more effectively. Secondly, there is a restructuring of the Superego and in particular of the Ego ideal in that a new introject is laid down as part of the process of regeneration. This introject is the image of Christ to which the individual now aspires and which he now seeks to emulate. The decision, which is a prerequisite to the entrance of the "Power from on high" is an Ego conscious and volitional decision. The entrance of the Holy Spirit and the πνεῦμα power from on high, also produces greater clarity of the ves-tigial consciousness and thus a clearer perception and appre-ciation of the law written on the heart. As previously indicated, the availability of πνεῦμα energy also gives the Ego the additional power necessary to live by the "cardiac law" which is now seen more clearly. Such are the essential psychotheo-logical differences between the saved and unsaved individual.

THE PSYCHOTHEOLOGY OF "POWER FROM ON HIGH"

"Power from on high" or πνεῦμα used with ἅγιον

This is one of the most important uses of the word

πνεῦμα   and it is at this point that tradition most often appears to replace exegesis and translation, with interpretation. It is, therefore, of importance that the psychotheological use of the phrase be examined. There are three types of this particular combination:

1) Neither word has the article.

2) Both words have the article.

3) One word has the article.

Since the Holy Spirit is the author of these words and since His works are perfect it is important that such differences be noted. It is in vain that the Divine author of Scripture has used " πνεῦμα ἅγιον   ," without any definite articles, and "the πνεῦμα the Holy," with two articles, if we neglect the distinction and render them both as the Holy Spirit meaning God the Holy Spirit.

An examination of the 50 passages where the expression " πνεῦμα ἅγιον " occurs indicates that it is probably never used of the Holy Spirit, for which " τὸ πνεῦμα τὸ ἅγιον" is most often used. The expression is used, rather, for the gifts given by the Holy Spirit or for what the Holy Spirit does. Thus in John 3:6 we read that "that which is born of the πνεῦμα (ἐκ τοῦ πνεύματος) is πνεῦμα , i.e., the gift.

The question remains as to what is the correct meaning of " πνεῦμα ἅγιον   ." To render it "Holy Spirit" is not much clearer. It is fortunate, however, that Christ Himself gave us the clue and leaves us in no doubt as to what is meant by " πνεῦμα ἅγιον   ." This is made clear by an examination of Acts. 1:4-5 with Luke 24:49.

In Acts 1:4-5 the Lord commanded the Apostles "that they should not depart from Jerusalem, but wait for the promise," (i.e., the fulfilment of the promise) "of the Father." They had heard the initial promise as it is recorded in Luke 24:49. "Behold, I send the Promise of my Father upon you: but tarry ye in the city of Jerusalem, until ye be endued with power from on high." This was the promise and it is further explained in Acts 1:5 in which the Lord adds that "John truely baptized with water; but ye shall be baptized with " πνεῦμα ἅγιον " not many days hence. In both of these passages the Lord is speaking of the same thing, namely, "the promise of the Father." In Luke 24:49 this promise is called "power from high," whereas in Acts 1:5 He calls the same promise " πνεῦμα ἅγιον ." Therefore, the conclusion is obvious that " πνεῦμα ἅγιον " is identical with "power from on high." This "power from on high" or πνεῦμα ἅγιον may be manifested in a variety of ways depending on the particular gift in question. Thus it may be power for tongues, power for miracles, power for wisdom, power for faith, etc. Thus the phrase " πνεῦμα ἅγιον " could better be rendered "Divine power," or "spiritual power" or "spiritual gifts" or, indeed, "power from on high."

It is noteworthy that Luke, himself, in his gospel in 1:3 claims to possess this very power "from above." The phrase which is tranlsated "from the very first" is ἄνωθεν and should be rendered "from above" as indeed it is in James 1:17. "Every good gift and every perfect gift cometh down from above." It

is also correctly rendered thus in a number of other places
in the New Testament.

It is thus questionable whether the phrase πνεῦμα ἅγιον
should ever be translated "Holy Spirit" but rather as His
Divine "power" as manifested in His operations and in His gifts.
We should always seek to distinguish the phrase πνεῦμα ἅγιον
from the πνεῦμα as, indeed they are carefully distinquished
in Acts 2:4. On that occasion, the Apostles "were all filled
with πνεῦμα ἅγιον , (the gift), and began to speak with
other tongues (one of his gifts) as the πνεῦμα (God the Holy
Spirit) gave them utterance."

It should also be noted that the Greek verb "to fill"
is always followed by the genitive case of that with which anything or anyone is filled. Thus in Acts 2:4, it is stated that
" ἐπλήσθησαν πάντες πνεύματος ἁγίου ." A similar construction
can be seen in numerous other places, e.g.:

     a) "filled with confusion" (of confusion) Acts. 19:29.

     b) "filled with indignation" (of indignation)
       Acts. 13:43.

     c) "filled with envy" (of envy) Acts. 13:52.

In all of these passages where filled is followed by
πνεῦμα ἅγιον in the genitive, there is no article in the
original and, it is suggested, that there should be none in
the English. On each occasion the genitive is used after the
verb "to fill" to indicate that with which they were filled,
i.e., with "power from on high" which is spiritual or Divine
power.

In connection with this same grammatical law it should also be noted that the accusative case is used of the place, person or thing which is filled. Thus in Acts 5:28 we read: " καὶ ἰδου πεπληρώκατε τηνʼΙερουσαλημ (accusative) τῆς διδακῆς (Genitive)ὑμῶν ." In addition, when the person, agent or instrument that fills is to be mentioned, then the dative case or the preposition (ἐν) followed by the dative is used. The article may be latent within the preposition and is not required to be separately introduced except for purposes of emphasis. This construction is seen in Ephesians 2:22. "Ye are build together for an habitation of God by or through the Spirit (ἐν πνεύματι), i.e., through the agency of God the Holy Spirit. Similarly in Ephesians 5:18 states, ἀλλα πλεροῦσθε ἐν πνεύματι , λαλοῦντες ἑαυτοις ψαλμοῖς καὶ ὕμνοις ," where we are exhorted to be filled not "with the Spirit" as is so commonly stated but "by the agency of God the Holy Spirit," the valid inference being "with power from on high." The Ephesian believers were not to be filled with or by wine, in which there is talkativeness, but by God the Holy Spirit who, fills with "power from on high" which is the basis for spiritual conversation. If the currently popular interpretation of this verse had validity then the word πνεῦμα would necessarily be in the genitive case. It will also be found that in the New Testament the same grammitical rule applies to the adjective "full."

Two other important verses must be examined within the context of these views. Firstly, in Acts 8:19-20, we read that Simon Magus made a request of Peter. "Give me also this power, than on whomsoever I lay hands, he may receive " πνεῦμα ἅγιον ." But Peter said unto him, thy money perish with thee, because thou hast thought that the gift of God may be purchased with money." This is not God the Holy Spirit but the gift of Divine power or God's gift. And as the gift of God, " πνεῦμα ἅγιον " can be spoken of as being received.

The second text of importance is John 20:22 where our Lord breathed on the Apostles and said, " λάβετε πνεῦμα ἅγιον ." It is important to note the absence of the article. In the opinion of this student, it was not God the Holy Spirit who was meant, for since Christ had not yet gone to the Father, He, The Holy Spirit, had not yet come (John 16:13). The verse rather means, "Receive ye power from on high," which is spiritual gifts or power. Thus an awareness of the exact words of Scripture helps to solve what would otherwise be a significant problem.

It should also be noted that on occasion the article is used grammatically to refer to an antecedent, without God the Holy Spirit being indicated (Acts 8:18 compared with Verses 15 and 16). Similarly the phrase "the πνεῦμα the ἅγιον " in Acts 11:15 refers to the gift of power from on high. The giver of the gift, God the Holy Spirit, is then noted in Verse 17. " ἐπέπεσεν τὸ πνεῦμα τὸ ἅγιον ἐπ'αὐτους ."

The psychotheological significance of these observations is, of course, that the augment which the new creature receives in regeneration is Divine power or energy, rather than a

"Person." As we have already seen, it is precisely such a supply of Divine energy that the new creature requires to augment his own psychic energy so that behaviors may be changed and a Christ exalting life may result.

BIBLIOGRAPHY

Articles

Blum, G. S. "A Study of the Psychoanalytic Theory of Psycho-
    sexual Development," Genetic Psychological Monographs.
    New York: International Universities Press, 39 (1952),
    3-99.

Bornstein, B. "On Latency," The Psychoanalytic Study of the
    Child. New York: International Universities Press, VI,
    1951.

Freud, A. "Adolescence," The Psychoanalytic Study of the Child.
    New York: International Universities Press, XIII, 1958.

Gould, E. P. "Spirit," The Biblical Encyclopaedia.

Harris, B. F. "Συνείδησις in the Pauline Writings," Westminister
    Theological Journal. No. 24-25, (1961), 173-186.

Hartman, H., and E. Kris. "Comments on the Formation of Psychic
    Structure," The Psychoanalytic Study of the Child. New
    York: International Universities Press, II, 1948.

_____, and R. M. Loewenstein. "Notes on the Superego,"
    The Psychoanalytic Study of the Child. New York:
    International Universities Press, XVII, 1962.

Howard, J. K. "The Concept of the Soul in Psychology and
    Religion," Journal of the American Scientific Affiliation.
    24, No. 4, December, 1972.

Jacobson, E. "The Self and the Object World," Psychoanalytic
    Study of the Child. New York: International Universities
    Press, IX, 1964.

Laidlaw, J. B. "Spirit," The Dictionary of the Bible, ed.
    J. Hastings. New York: Charles Scribner's Sons, (1930),
    612.

Lampl-de-Groot, J. "Ego Ideal and Superego," Psychoanalytic
    Study of the Child. New York: International Universities
    Press, XVII (1961), 94-108.

Laufer, M. "Ego Ideal and Pseudo Ego Ideal in Adolescence,"
    Psychoanalytic Study of the Child. New York: International
    Universities Press, XIS, 1964.

Murray, J. M. "Narcissism and the Ego Ideal," Journal of the American Psychoanalytic Association. 37 (1964), 106-121.

Nunberg, H. "The Synthetic Function of the Ego," and "The Feeling of Guilt," The Practice and Theory of Psychoanalysis. New York: International Universities Press, Chapters VIII and IX, 1948.

Osborne, H. "Conscience in the New Testament," Journal of Theological Studies. XXXII, 167-179.

A Psychiatric Glossary, Committee on Public Information of the American Psychiatric Association, Washington D. C. (1964), 38.

Reich, A. "Early Identifications and Superego," The International Journal of Psychoanalysis. 18, (1954), 76-89.

Sandler, J. "The Classification of Superego Material," Psychoanalytic Study of the Child. New York: International Universities Press, XVIII, 1962.

_____. "On the Concept of Superego," The Psychoanalytic Study of the Child. New York: International Universities Press, XV, 1960.

_____, A. Holder, and D. Meers. "The Ego Ideal and the Ideal Self," Psychoanalytic Study of the Child. New York: International Universities Press, XVIII, 1963.

Books

Anderson, F. Die Seele un das Gewissen. Leipzig, Germany: Felix Meiner Verlag, 1929, p. 54.

Arlow, J. A., and C. Brenner, Psychoanalytic Concepts and Structural Theory. New York: International Universities Press, 1964.

Baird, Thomas. Conscience. New York: Charles C. Cook, 1914, p. 19.

Baldwin, Joseph. Elementary Psychology and Education. London: Appleton and Co., 1893, pp. 241-253.

Bergler, E. The Superego. New York: Grune and Stratton, 1952, p. 7.

Berkhof, L. Systematic Theology. Grand Rapids, 1941, pp. 191 ff.

216

Bigg, C. The Christian Platonists of Alexandra. Oxford, 1968.

Bullinger, E. W., ed. The Companion Bible. Appendix 13, London: Humphrey Wilford, Oxford University Press, P. 19.

_____. A Critical Lexicon and Concordance to the English and Greek New Testament. London: The Lamp Press, Ltd.

Calvin, John. Institutes of the Christian Religion. Grand Rapids, Erdmans, 1, No. 15, 1957.

Carmichael, L. Manual of Child Psychology. New York: John Wiley and Sons, 1946, p. 739.

Carrington, W. L. Psychology, Religion and Human Need. London, 1957, p. 40.

Chafer, L. S. Systematic Theology. Dallas Seminary Press, 1964, pp. 146-147.

Charles, R. H. A Critical History of the Doctrine of the Future Life. p. 152.

Cohu, J. R. Vital Problems of Religion. Edinburgh: T. & T. Clark, 1914, p. 199.

Cremer, Hermann. Biblico-Theological Lexicon of New Testament Greek. Translated from the German of the second edition. Edinburgh: T. & T. Clark, 1878.

Cullman, O. Immortality of the Soul or Resurrection of the Dead. London, 1958, p. 19.

Delitzsch, F. A System of Biblical Psychology. Edinburgh: T. & T. Clark, 1867, p. 92.

de M. Sajous, C. E. Strength of Religion as Shown by Science. Philadelphia: F. A. Davis Co., 1914, p. 221.

Eidelberg, L. A Comparative Pathology of the Neuroses. New York: International Universities Press, 1954, pp. 99-102.

Emerson, W. Outline of Psychology. Wheaton, Illinois: Van Kampen Press, Inc., 1953, p. 428.

Engel, G. Psychological Development in Health and Disease. London: W. B. Saunders Co., 1962, pp. 141-154.

Fenichel, O. The Psychoanalytic Theory of Neurosis. New York: W. W. Norton, 1945, p. 186.

Freud, S. The Ego and the Id. Standard Edition. London: Hogarth Press, 1923, p. 187.

_____. *The Ego and the Id*. Standard Edition. London: Hogarth Press, XIX, 1957, p. 87.

_____. *Ego and Mechanisms of Defense*. New York: International Universities Press, 1946.

_____. *A General Introduction to Psychoanalysis*. London: Liveright, 1935, p. 371.

_____. *Group Psychology and the Analysis of the Ego*. London: Hogarth Press, 1922.

_____. *Introductory Lectures*. Standard Edition. London: Hogarth Press, 1917, p. 107.

_____. *New Introductory Lectures*. New York: Norton, 1933.

_____. *On Narcissism*. Standard Edition. London: Hogarth Press, 1914.

_____. *An Outline of Psychoanalysis*. Standard Edition. London: Hogarth Press, 1938, pp. 89-90.

_____. *The Problem of Anxiety*. New York: Norton Co., 1936, p. 125.

Foster, A. D. *The New Dimensions of Religion*. New York: The MacMillan Co., 1931, p. 176.

Froom, Edwin. *The Conditionalist Faith of our Fathers*. Review and Herald Publishing Association, I, 1950.

_____. *Man for Himself*. New York: Rinehart, 1947.

Girdlestone, R. B. *Synonyms of the Old Testament*. Grand Rapids: Wm. B. Erdmans Publishing Company, 1941.

Grenfell, B. P. *The Oxyrhynchus Papyri*. London: Kegan, Paul, Trench, Trubner & Co., II,III,VI, VIII, XI, XIII, XV, 1899 and 1903.

_____, P. Bernard, Hunt, S. Arthur, Smyly, and J. Gilbart. *The Tebtunis Papyri*. London: Henry Frowde, I, 1902.

Hallesby, O. *Conscience*. London: Inter-Varsity Fellowship, 1955.

Healy, W., A. F. Bronner, and A. M. Bowers. *The Structure and Meaning of Psychoanalysis*. New York: Knopf, 1940.

Homer, *Iliad*. Vol. V, IX, XXIII.

Hort, F. J. A. *Commentary on I Peter*. p. 134.

Jacobson, E. The Self and The Object World. New York: International Universities Press, 1954.

Josephus. Antiquities. English Translation by H. St. J. Thackery. New York: Putnams' Sons, XIII, 1939.

Josselyn, I. M. The Adolescent and His World. New York: Family Service Association of America, 1952.

Jowett, Benjamin. (Translator). The Dialogues of Plato.

_____. Plato's Timaeus. The Library of Liberal Arts, No. 14, pp. 52-53.

Kirk, K. E. Conscience and Its Problems. London: Longmans, Green & Co., n.d., p. 3.

Kittel. Theological Dictionary of the New Testament. VI, IX, pp. 336-347 and pp. 609-646.

Klein, M. The Psychoanalysis of Children. London: Hogarth Press, 1949.

Koehler, L., and Walter Baumgartner, eds. Lexicon in Veteris Testamenti Libros. II, pp. 626-627.

Lake, Kirsopp. (Translation), The Apostolic Fathers. London: William Heinemann, Vol. I, I Clement, II Clement, Ignatius, Plycarp, Didache, Barnabas. 1919.

Lampl-de-Groot, J. The Development of the Mind. New York: International Universities Press, 1965, pp. 114-125.

Laughlin, H. P. Mental Mechanisms. Washington D. C.: Butterworths, 1963, pp. 1-26.

McDougall, William. Character and Conduct of Life. Boston: Putnam, 1927, p. 148.

Nelson, H. Adaption-Level Theory: An Experimental and Systematic Approach to Behavior. New York, 1964, p. 541.

Niebuhr, R. The Nature and Destiny of Man. New York: Charles Scribner's Sons, 1955, p. 150.

Perrin, Bernadotte. (Translation), Plutarch's Lives. London: William Heinemann, Vol. VI, Dion and Brutus, Timoleon and Aemulus Paulus, 1918, pp. 206-209.

Perrin, Bernadotte. (Translation), Plutarch's Lives. London: William Heinemann, Vol. VIII, Sertorius and Eumenes, Phocion and Cato the Younger, 1919, pp. 140.

Perrin, Bernadotte. (Translation), Plutarch's Lives. London: William Heinemann, Vol. XI, Aratus, Artaxeres, Galba, and Otho, 1926.

Perrin, Bernadotte. (Translation), Plutarch's Moralia. London: William Heinemann, Vol. II, IV.

Philo. The Law of Allegory. I.S., p. 22.

Pierce, C. A. Conscience in the New Testament. London: SCM Press Ltd., 1955.

Piers, G., and M. Singer. Shame and Guilt. Springfield: Thomas Press, 1953.

Rehwinkel, A. M. "Conscience," Baker's Dictionary of Theology. Grand Rapids, 1960, p. 136.

Richardson, A., ed. "Conscience," A Theological Word Book of the Bible. London: SCM Press, 1950, p. 83.

_____, ed. "Mind, Heart," A Theological Word Book of the Bible. London: SCM Press, 1950, p. 144.

Stuart, G. Conscience and Reason. London: George Allen and Unwin, Ltd., 1951, p. 162.

Thorndike, E. L. Educational Psychology. New York: Columbia University, 1913, p. 202.

Valentine, Milton. Christian Theology. Philadelphia: The United Lutheran Publication House, I, 1906, pp. 385-393.

Vaughan, F. W. General Psychology. New York: The Odyssey Press, 1939, p. 272.

Woodworth, R. S., and D. G. Marquis. Psychology. New York: Henry Holt and Co., 1947, p. 141.

Xenophon. Cyropaedia. Loeb Classical Library. London: G. B. Putnam's Sons, Vol. IV, No. 4, p. 10.

CPSIA information can be obtained at www.ICGtesting.com
Printed in the USA
LVOW03s2330090115

422173LV00003BA/3/P

9 781935 434672